MOBILE COMPUTING

A STUDY MATERIAL OF BHARATHIAR UNIVERSITY

MURUGANANTHAM P YUVARAJ S ARUN JOSEPH A

Dedicated to the God Almighty my creator, my strong pillar, my source of inspiration, wisdom, knowledge and understanding. He has been the source of my strength throughout this program and on His wings only have I soared. I also dedicate this work to my friends and family members who have encouraged me all the way and whose encouragement has made sure that I give it all it takes to finish that which I have started. And also, my sincere dedication to all creators of these materials helped me to consolidate and create this study material for the rural students of Bharathiar University.

Thank you.

Contents

Preface

UNIT I:

Introduction: Mobility of Bits and Bytes –Wireless The Beginning – Mobile Computing – Dialogue Control – Networks – Middleware and Gateways – Application and services- Developing Mobile computer Applications – security in mobile computing – Standards _ Why is it necessary – Standard bodies. MOBILE COMPUTTING ARCHITECTURE: History of computers and Internet – Architecture for mobile computing – Three-tier architecture – Design considerations for mobile computing – Mobile computing through Internet – Making exiting applications mobile enabled

UNIT II:

MOBILE COMPUTING THROUGH TELEPHONY: Evaluation of telephony – Multiple access procedures – Mobile computing through telephone – IVR Application – Voice XML – TAPI

UNIT III:

EMERGING TECHNOLOGIES: Blue Tooth – RFID – WiMAX – Mobile IP – IPv6 – Java Card. GSM : Global System for mobile communications – GSM Architecture – GSM Entities – Call routing in GSM – PLMN Interfaces – GSM Addresses and Identifiers – Network Aspects in GSM – GSM Frequency allocations – Authentications and Security. SMS

UNIT IV:

GPRS – GPRS and packet data network – GPRS network architecture – GPRS network operations – Data services in GPRS – Application for GPRS- Limitations – Billing and Charging. WAP : MMS – GPRS Applications

UNIT V:

CDMA and 3G: Spread spectrum technology – Is 95 – CDMA vs GSM – Wireless Data – Third generation networks – Applications on 3G WIRELESS LAN: Wireless LAN advantages – IEEE 802.11 standards – Architecture – Mobile in Wireless LAN – Deploying wireless LAN – Mobile adhoc networks and sensor networks – Wireless LAN Security – WiFi vs 3G

Acknowledgements

I owe special thanks to the entire team of publishers. Their suggestions have helped in making the study material more useful. This book is an attempt to collect the materials of various subjects from various materials to help the studnts to easily develop their knowledge. I would advise readers to take advantage of this work to the fullest extent possible.

CHAPTER I

INTRODUCTION

MOBILE COMPUTING

Mobile computing refers to using the small portable and hand held computing devices such as PDA, laptops, mobile phones, MP3 players, digital cameras, tablet PC and Palmtops in a wireless enabled network.

MOBILITY OF BITS AND BYTES

Mobility of physical object related to movement of matters, mobility of virtual objects related to mobility of bits and bytes.

- In the last two centuries, mobility has been redefined.
- Both physical and virtual objects are now mobile.
    - Mobility of physical objects relate to movement of matters, whereas movements of virtual objects relate to movements of bits and bytes

- The US formed the Advanced Research Projects Agency (ARPA) within the Department of Defense (DoD).
- This laid the foundation of packet switched data networks.
- The important ones are TCP /IP and X.25.
    - TCP/*IP* was driven by education and defense in the USA
    - Whereas X.25 was driven by European telecommunication industry and Governments.

The Convergence Leading to ICT

The first step towards the convergence between telecommunication and IT happened in 1965 when AT&T used computers to do the switching in Electronic switching system (ESS). On the other hand packet switch network was bringing communication closer to computer.

The World Wide Web (WWW), which was started by Tim Berners-Lee in 1989 as text processing software, bought these two faculties of technology together and established internet as a powerful media.

The internet meets four primary needs of the society: communication, knowledge sharing, commerce, and entertainment. This convergence is called information and communication technologies (ICT).

ICT will address the need to access data, information, and knowledge from anywhere, anytime.

WIRELESS-THE BEGINNING

- In 1947 researchers in AT&T Bell Labs conceived the idea of cellular phones.
- They realized that by using small service areas or cells they can reuse the frequency.
- This in turn can enhance the traffic capacity of mobile phones.

- AT&T requested the Federal Communication Commission (FCC) to allocate a large number of radio-spectrum frequencies so that widespread mobile telephone service would become feasible.
- Every country has its own regulatory agencies lice FCC.

Evolution of Wireless Network

The first wireless network was commissioned in Germany in 1958. It was called A-Netz and used analog technology at 160MHz. only outgoing calls were possible in this network.

This system evolved into B-Netz operating at the same 160MHz. It was possible to receive an incoming call from a fixed telephone network.

Evolution of Wireless Data

First generation (1G):

- Uses analogue signal.
- Uses frequency division multiple access for modulation (FDMA).
- EG. AMPS(advanced mobile phone)

Second generation (2G):

- Uses digitized technology.
- Uses time division multiple access for modulation and FDMA.
- EG. CDMA

In 1G and 2G the data are transacted over circuits and called circuit switch data.

2.5G:

- Uses digitized technology.
- Data transferred by packets.
- EG. GPRS

3.3G:

- Uses quantum leap technology.
- Uses spread spectrum technology and media access techniques for encoding.
- Data and voice are transferred by packets.

EG- UMTS & CDMA2000. The domain of wireless network today is,

- Wireless PAN (Bluetooth, Infrared).
- Wireless LAN
- Wireless WAN

DIALOGUE CONTROL:

In communication there are two types of user dialogues.

1. Long session
2. Short session

- Going through monolithic document page by page is session oriented.
- Going to the particular page through index can be short transaction.

- Session: it is helpful in services offered through computers with large screens and mouse
- Short: It may be desired for devices with input and output like SMS.

Example:

A bank balance enquiry over internet.

Session:
1. Enter the URL of bank website.
2. Enter the acc number and password to login.
3. See the balance by entering the enquiry dialogue.
4. Logout the internet Banking

- Short: A user can send a SMS message say "My Bal" to the system and receives the information on balance.

NETWORKS:

A group of two or more computer systems linked together. There are many types of computer networks, including:

- Local-area networks (LANs): The computers are geographically close together (that is, in the same building).
- Wide-area networks (WANs): The computers are farther apart and are connected by telephone lines or radio waves.

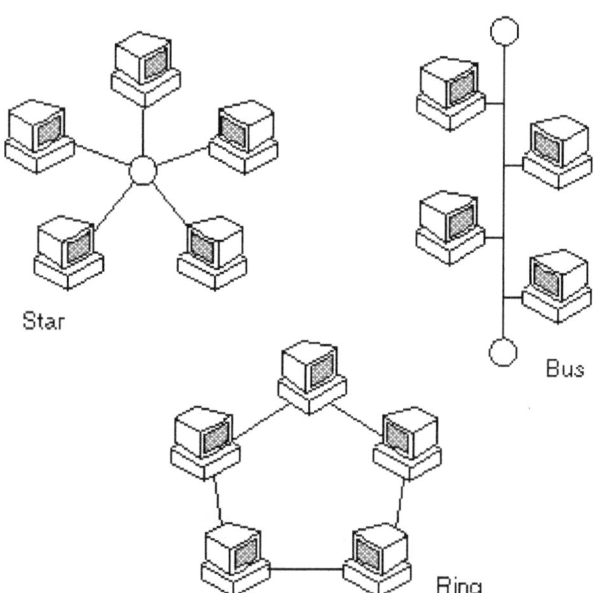

- Campus-area networks (CANs): The computers are within a limited geographic area, such as a campus or military base.
- Metropolitan-area networks (MANs): A data network designed for a town or city.
- Home-area networks (HANs): A network contained within a user's home that connects a person's digital devices.

Ad-hoc Network:

Ad-hoc network is a small area network, especially with wireless or temporary plug-in connection.

Bearers:

These were the message carrier or a equipment. Different types of bearer are used for different network.

MIDDLEWARE & GATEWAYS:

Software layered between a user agent and operating system is called as middleware. There are different types of middleware and gateways. They are,

Communication middleware's are,

1. Transaction processing middleware.
2. Behaviour management middleware.
3. Communication gateways.

1. Communication middleware.

- The application will communicate with different nodes and services through different communication middleware.
- Different **connectors** for different services will fall in this category.

2. Transaction processing middleware.

- In many cases a service will offer session oriented dialogue (SoD).
- For a session we need to maintain a state over the stateless Internet.
- This is done through an application server

3. Behaviour management middleware.

- For different devices we need different types of rendering.
- We can have applications, which are developed specially for different types of rendering.
- For example, we can have one application for Web, another for WAP, and a different one for SMS.

4. Communication gateways.

- Between the device and the middleware there will be network of networks.
- Gateways are deployed when there are different transport bearers or networks with dissimilar protocols.

For example, we need an IVR (Interactive Voice Response) gateway to interface voice with a computer, or a WAP gateway to access internet over a mobile phone.

In a communications network, a network node equipped for interfacing with another network that uses different protocols.

- A gateway may contain devices such as protocol translators, impedance matching devices, rate converters, fault isolators, or signal translators as necessary to provide system interoperability.
- It also requires the establishment of mutually acceptable administrative procedures between both networks.
- A protocol translation/mapping gateway interconnects networks with different network protocol technologies by performing the required protocol conversions.

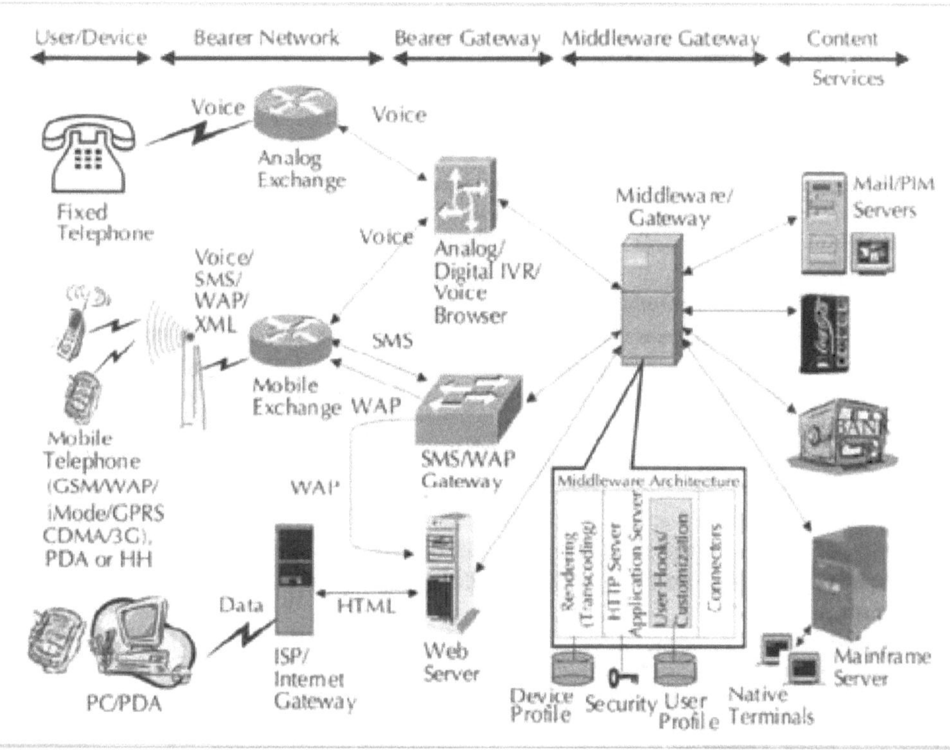

A Schematic representation of Mobile Computing Environment

APPLICATION AND SERVICES:

There may be many applications and services for mobile computing space. These services run on origin server its also known as content servers.

The general application of mobile are,

- Personal-belongs to user.
- Perishable-time sensitive relevance passes quickly.
- Transaction Oriented-transactions need to be closed
- Location Specific-Information related to current geographic location.
- Business information-corporate business information.
- Entertainment-application for fun, entertainment.
- News-basket of applications having different types of news.
- Weather report-about nature and climate.

DEVELOPING MOBILE COMPUTING APPLICATIONS:

- Any portal system today supports user mobility. The E-mail account can also be checked even in mobility. Internet can be accessed anywhere and anytime.
- The context and behaviour adaptation is required to provide a service that is tailored to user's presentation.
- **Mobile application development** is the process by which application software is developed for low-power handheld devices, such as personal digital assistants, enterprise digital assistants or mobile phones.
- These applications can be pre-installed on phones during manufacturing, downloaded by customers from various mobile software distribution platforms, or delivered as web applications using server-side or client-side

processing (e.g. JavaScript) to provide an "application-like" experience within a Web browser.

- Application software developers also have to consider a lengthy array of screen sizes, hardware specifications and configurations because of intense competition in mobile software and changes within each of the platforms.

SECURITY IN MOBILE COMPUTING:

- Security implementation should be device independent, network independent, bearer independent. Security must be end-to-end security.
- Java Card technology was originally developed for the purpose of securing sensitive information stored on smart cards. Security is determined by various aspects of this technology:

- **Data encapsulation.** Data is stored within the application, and Java Card applications are executed in an isolated environment (the Java Card VM), separate from the underlying operating system and hardware.
- **Applet Firewall.** Unlike other Java VMs, a Java Card VM usually manages several applications, each one controlling sensitive data. Different applications are therefore separated from each other by an applet firewall which restricts and checks access of data elements of one applet to another.
- **Cryptography**. Commonly used encryption algorithms like DES, Triple DES, AES, RSA (including elliptic curve cryptography) are supported.
- **Applet.** The applet is a state machine which processes only incoming command requests and responds by sending data or response status words back to the interface device.

STANDARDS:

- Standards are documented agreements containing technical specifications or other precise.
- Standards ensure that material, products, processes and services fit for their defined and agreed purpose.

Who makes the standard?

- Based on the operation standard bodies are formed by government, professional institute or industry consortiums.
- In India, standard bodies are under the government called bureau of Indian standard or BIS.

Some standard bodies:

- ISO

1.It is nongovernmental organisation established in 1947.
2. One of the most widely known standards from ISO is ISO9000.

- IETF

1. Internet Engineering Task Force (IETF).
2. It is an open international community for Network Designers, operators, vendors and researches concerned with smooth operation of internet.
3. The standards for email is defined in RFC821 (SMTP).

- ETSI

1. European Telecommunication Standard Institute(ETSI)
2. Major Roleàdeveloping wide range of standards and technical documentation.
3. ObjectiveàSupport global harmonisation by providing forum.

- OMA

1.Open Mobile Alliance established by consolidation of WAP Forum.
2. It supports easy to use mobile experience for end users.

- ITU

1.International Telecommunication union (ITU).
2. Mission is to provide efficient and on time production of high quality standards in all fields of Telecommunication

- IEEE

1.International Standards Association(IEEE-SA)à
2. Produce standards which are developed internationally.
3. It supports industry-led consensus process and operating procedures and guidelines.

- W3C

1.World Wide Web Consortium (W3C) is a forum for information , commerce, communication and collective understanding.
2. It contributes standardized web technologies by producing specifications.
3. W3C recommendations include HTML, XML, CSS, Web services, DOM (Document Object Model) etc...

Players in the Wireless Space:

The players in WLAN are,

1. Regulatory Authority
2. Service provider
3. User
4. Equipment Vendors
5. Research organization
6. Survey of sites
7. Location of base station.
8. Mobile switching centre
9. Base station controller, Base transceiver station ,cells

MOBILE COMPUTING ARCHITECTURE:

History of computers and internet:

- The Internet is the largest internet in the world. It is a three level hierarchy composed of backbone networks (e.g. Arpanet, NSFNet, and MILNET), mid-level networks, and stub networks.
- These include commercial (.com or .co), university (.ac or .edu) and other research networks (.org, .net) and military (.mil) networks and span many different physical networks around the world with various protocols, chiefly the Internet Protocol

Computer History Year/Enter	Inventors/Inventions
1936	Konrad Zuse - Z1 Computer
1942	John Atanasoff & Clifford Berry ABC Computer
1944	Howard Aiken & Grace Hopper Harvard Mark I Computer
1946	John Presper Eckert & John W. Mauchly ENIAC 1 Computer
1948	Frederic Williams & Tom Kilburn Manchester Baby Computer & The Williams Tube
1947/48	John Bardeen, Walter Brattain & Wiliam Shockley The Transistor
1951	John Presper Eckert & John W. Mauchly UNIVAC Computer
1953	International Business Machines IBM 701 EDPM Computer
1954	John Backus & IBM FORTRAN Computer Programming Language
1962	Steve Russell & MIT Space war Computer Game
1964	Douglas Engelhard Computer Mouse & Windows
1969	Arpanet
1970	Intel 1103 Computer Memory
1971	Fagin, Hoff & Mazor Intel 4004 Computer Microprocessor
1971	Alan Shugart &IBM The "Floppy" Disk
1973	Robert Metcalfe & Xerox The Ethernet Computer Networking
1974/75	Scelbi & Mark-8 Altair & IBM 5100 Computers
1976/77	Apple I, II & TRS-80 & Commodore Pet Computers
1978	Dan Bricklin & Bob Frankston VisiCalc Spreadsheet Software

ARCHITECTURE FOR MOBILE COMPUTING:
THREE-TIER ARCHITECTURE:

- Three-tier is a client–server architecture in which the user interface, functional process logic , computer data storage and data access are developed and maintained as independent modules, most often on separate platforms.
- The three-tier model is a software architecture and a software design pattern.
- Apart from the usual advantages of modular software with well-defined interfaces, the three-tier architecture is intended to allow any of the three tiers to be upgraded or replaced independently as requirements or technology change.
- For example, a change of operating system in the presentation tier would only affect the user interface code.
- Typically, the user interface runs on a desktop PC or workstation and uses a standard graphical user interface, functional process logic may consist of one or more separate modules running on a workstation or application server, and an RDBMS on a database server or mainframe contains the computer data storage logic.

Three-tier architecture has the following three tiers:

Presentation tier:

1. This is the topmost level of the application.
2. The presentation tier displays information related to such services as browsing merchandise, purchasing, and shopping cart contents. It communicates with other tiers by outputting results to the browser/client tier and all other tiers in the network.

Application tier

(Business logic, logic tier, data access tier, or middle tier):

1. The logic tier is pulled out from the presentation tier and, as its own layer; it controls an application's functionality by performing detailed processing.

We can group middleware into major categories.

1. **Message oriented middleware.**

- **It** is software or hardware infrastructure supporting sending and receiving messages between distributed systems.
- MOM allows application modules to be distributed over heterogeneous platforms and reduces the complexity of developing applications that span multiple operating systems and network protocols.
- MOM provides software elements that reside in all communicating components of client/server architecture and typically support asynchronous calls between the client and server applications.

2. Transaction processing (TP) middleware:

- It provides a tool and an environment for developing transaction-based distributed application.
- It is used in data management, network access, security systems, airline reservations etc..,
- TP middleware maps numerous client requests through application-service routines to different application tasks.

3. Communication middleware:

- A communication middleware framework provides an environment that enables two applications to set up a conversation and exchange data. Typically, this exchange of data will involve the triggering of one or more transactions along the way

4. Distributed Objects and Components:

- Distributed Objects are supported by an Object Request Broker (ORB), which manages the communication and data exchange with (potentially) remote objects.
- ORBs are based on the concept of *Interoperable Object References*, which facilitate the remote creation, location, invocation, and deletion of objects often involving object factories and other helper objects.,
- The most common ORB implementations are CORBA, COM/DCOM, and RMI. While RMI is limited to Java and COM/DCOM is restricted to Microsoft platforms,
- CORBA spans multiple platforms and programming languages.

5. Trans coding middleware:

- It is used to transfer one format of data to another format to suite the need of the client.

E.g.: trans coding the HTML page into WML page.

Data tier:

1. This tier consists of database servers. Here information is stored and retrieved.
2. This tier keeps data neutral and independent from application servers or business logic. Giving data its own tier also improves scalability and performance.

Database Middleware:

- This type of middleware allows for direct access to databases, and provides direct interaction with databases.
- There are many database gateways and connectivity options, and you simply have to see what will best work for your necessary solution.
- This is the most general and commonly known type of middleware. This includes SQL database software.

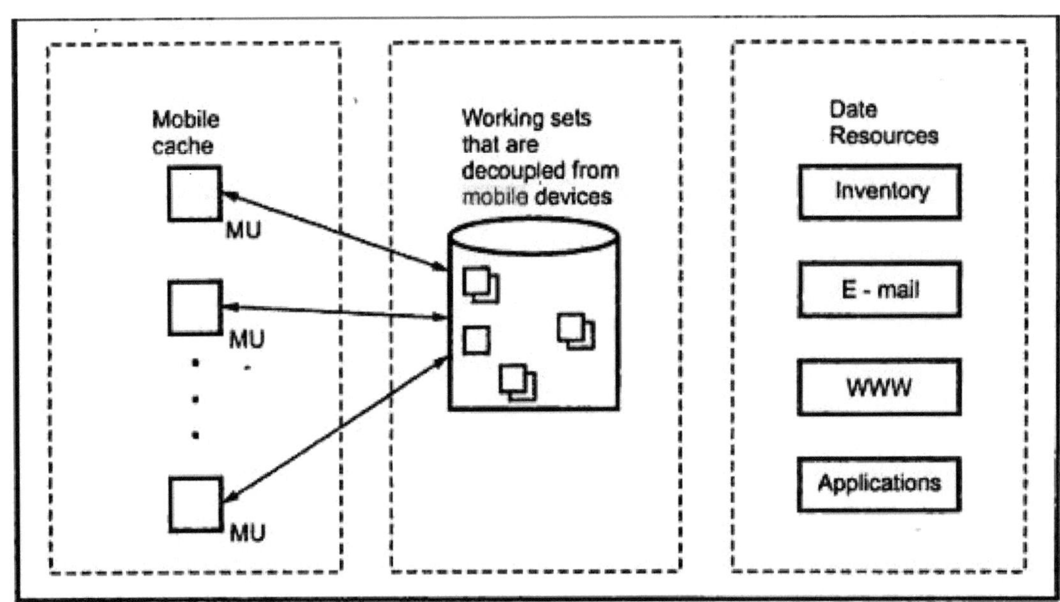

FIG. Three-tier architecture

SyncML:

- **SyncML (Synchronization Markup Language)** is the former name for a platform-independent information synchronization standard..
- The purpose of Sync ML is to offer an open standard as a replacement for existing data synchronization solutions, which have mostly been somewhat vendor-, application- or operating system specific.
- The new version of the specification includes support for push email, providing a standard protocol alternative to proprietary solutions like BlackBerry.

Several major companies such as Samsung, Motorola, Nokia, Sony Ericsson, LG, IBM and Siemens AG already support SyncML in their products.

DESIGN CONSIDERATIONS FOR MOBILE COMPUTING:

The mobile computing environment needs to be context independent as well as context sensitive.

Requirement of context management:

1. Context sensing
2. Context representation
3. Context interpretation

Composite capabilities / preference profiles:

- Cc/pp is proposed w3c standard for describing device capabilities and user preferences.
- A cc/pp profile contains a number of attribute names and associated values that are used by an application to determine appropriate form of a resource to deliver to a client.

Policy Manager:

- Policy manager is responsible for containing policies related to mobility.
- A policy is a set of rules. These rules follow different conditions.

Semantic web:

- It is a idea of having data on the web defined and linked in a way that it can be used by machines not just for display purposes but for automation, security, filtering, integration and reuse of data.

Security Manager:

It provides secure connection between the client device and the origin server

- Confidentially
- Integrity
- Availability
- Non-repudiation
- Trust

Platform for privacy preference project:

- P3p is an emerging standard defined by w3c.
- p3p enables concerns to express their privacy policies in standardized format so it can be retrieved and interpreted by user agents.

Attributes:

- Physical capability of the device.
- Logical capability.
- Network bandwidth
- Payload

Classification of Trans coding:

- Spatial trans coding
- Temporal trans coding
- Colour trans coding
- Code trans coding
- Object or semantic Trans coding.

Content aggregation:

There are two types of content aggregation,

- Single service request
- Group service request

<u>MOBILE COMPUTING THROUGH INTERNET:</u>

àTo support mobile computing over the Internet, two possible approaches can be considered.

1. One is to use mobile version of IP (Internet Protocol), which could support typical Internet applications.

2. The second approach is to use Wireless ATM (Asynchronous Transfer Mode), an emerging technology where ATM cells are transmitted over wireless links and part of the ATM connection lies in the wireless network.

àWireless ATM has received attention due to the need to support mobile multimedia services and also because of an increasing deployment of ATM technology in the Internet and other networks.

<u>MAKING EXISTING APPLICATIONS MOBILE ENABLED:</u>

There are many applications that are now being used within the intranet or the corporate network. These application need to be made ubiquitous and mobile computing possible. There are many ways by which this can be achieved:

- Enhance the existing application as current application: Enhance the application to support mobile computing.

- Rent an application from ASP, there are many organizations who develop ubiquitous application and rent the same at a fee.
- Write a new application; develop a new application to meet the new business requirement of the mobile computing.
- Buy a packaged solution, there are many companies who are offering packaged solutions for various business areas starting from manufacturing to sales and marketing. Buy and install one.
- Bridge the gap between middleware, use different middleware techniques to facelift and mobile computing enable the existing application.

CHAPTER II

MOBILE COMPUTING THROUGH TELEPHONY

EVOLUTION OF TELEPHONY:

- The first telephone system was developed by Alexander graham bell.
- There is a two way communication between two individuals in two locations

E.g.: calling or A party -------- the person makes a call
Called or B party---------- the person who responds to the call.

- In early 1980, the automatic telephone exchange was developed. It is called as "strowger switch".
- The first version of automatic telephone exchange was installed in 1892 a1 La Porte, indania, USA.
- In 1960 the first switching system was developed by AT&T.
- In 1960 and 1970 saw the advent of telephone exchanges that were controlled by processor and software (digital computer).this was called program control exchanges.
- In 1962 major mile stone was achieved when the system was made digital (transmitting the data's in digital form along with encoded format).
- A series of distinct tone is generated by a machine called "Ring Generator".
- The tones produced are,

  - Dial tone-the signal is applied to the line after the calling party has Lifted his handset and switching the equipment has allocated him for a call proceeds.

  - Busy tone- that the called subscriber is already busy.
  - Ring tone-circuit between a party and b party is established.

- A normal telephone system is called Public switched telephone network (PSTN).
- PSTN divided into three categories,

  - Local exchanges- used for connection of subscribers.
  - Transit exchanges-switch traffic between and within geographical area.
  - International exchanges- switch traffic in foreign countries.

MULTIPLE ACCESS PROCEDURES:

- In a PSTN network, a separate physical wire is used to connect the subscriber's telephone with the switch.
- Multiple users can communicate at same time.
- Radio channel is used in wireless network is shared by different users.

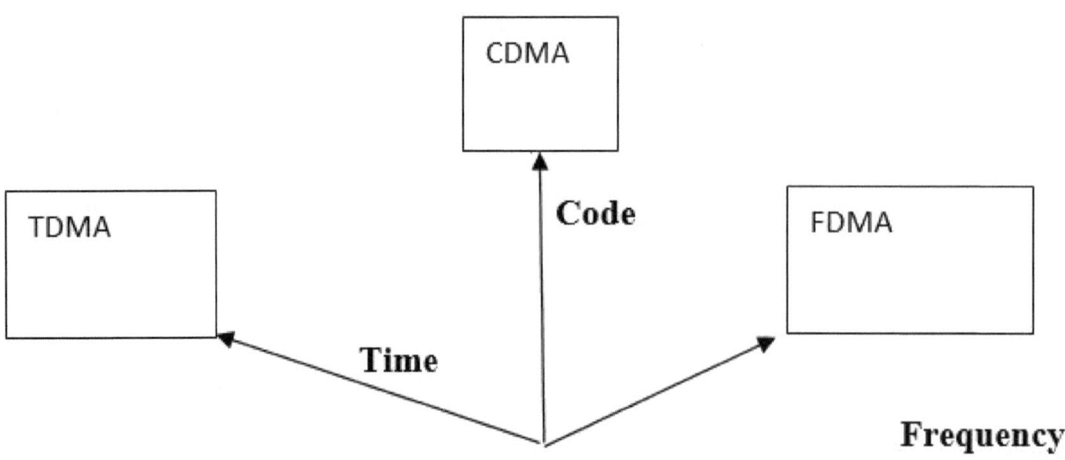

Frequency Division Multiple Accesses (FDMA):

- FDMA is one of the most common multiplexing procedures.
- The available frequency band is divided into channels of equal bandwidth so that each communication is carried on a different frequency.
- This multiplexing technique is used in all first generation analog in all first generation analog mobile networks.

Time Division Multiple Accesses (TDMA):

- TDMA is expense when compared to FDMA.
- GSM uses both TDMA and FDMA.
- A frequency range of 25 MHz holds 124 single channels of 200 kHz each, each frequency channel contains 8 TDMA conversation channel.

Code Division Multiple Accesses (CDMA):

- CDMA is broadband system
- It uses spread spectrum technology where each subscriber uses the whole bandwidth.
- All subscriber uses same frequency in CDMA.
- To separate signal each subscriber is assigned an orthogonal code called "CHIP".

Space Division Multiple Accesses (SDMA):

- SDMA is a technique where we use different part of space for multiplexing.
- SDMA is used in radio transmission and more useful in satellite communications to optimize the use of radio spectrum by using directional properties of antennas.

MOBILE COMPUTING THROUGH TELEPHONE:
IVR Application:
IVR PROGRAMMING:

Interactive voice response (IVR) is a technology that allows a computer to interact with humans through the use of voice and DTMF tones input via keypad.

- Voice technology encompasses the processing and manipulation of an audio signal in a Computer Technology (CT) system.
- It supports filtering, analysing, recording, compressing, storing, etc..,
- Voice driverà to communicate and control the voice hardware on the IVR system.
- The voice libraries are:

1. Libdxxmt.lib- the main voice library.
2. Libsrlmt.lib- the standard run-time library.

- The C function libraries are used to:

1. Utilize all the voice board features of call management.
2. Configure devices.
3. Handle events that occur on the devices.
4. Return device information.
5. Gather call transaction details.

IVR Application:

- IVR applications are programs that control and respond to calls on the IVR platform.
- IVR applications can either be developed by an enterprise, by an IVR development shop, or by companies that offer canned IVR applications.
- IVR applications direct the IVR platform to prompt callers, gather input, and transfer callers to other phones.
- IVR applications also call on existing back-end database and application servers to retrieve records and information required during the course of a call.
- VR platforms are the "server and operating system" hardware and software platforms on which IVR solutions run.
- IVR platforms at a minimum provide the ability to play and record prompts and gather touch-tone input.
- IVR platforms may also offer the ability to recognize spoken input from callers (voice recognition), translate text into spoken output for callers (text-to-speech), and transfer IVR calls to any telephone or call center agent.

IVR example:

File Voicent.cs:

```
using System;
using System.Net;
using System.IO;
Namespace Voicent
{
Public class Voicent
{
Public Voicent()
{
m_host = "localhost";
m_port = 8155;
}
Public Voicent(string
```

```
host, int port)
{
m_host = host;
m_port = port;
}
Public string CallText (string
phoneno, string text, bool selfdelete)
{
// call request url
string urlstr = "/ocall/callreqHandler.jsp";
// setting the http post string
string poststr = "info=Simple Text Call " +
phoneno;
poststr += "&phoneno=" + phoneno;
poststr += "&firstocc=10";
poststr += "&selfdelete=";
poststr += (selfdelete ? "1" : "0");
poststr += "&txt=" + text;
// Send Call Request
String rcstr = PostToGateway(urlstr, poststr);
return GetRequestID(rcstr);
}
public string CallAudio(string
phoneno, string filename, bool selfdelete)
{
// call request url
string urlstr = "/ocall/callreqHandler.jsp";
// setting the http post string
string poststr = "info=Simple Audio Call " +
phoneno;
poststr += "&phoneno=" + phoneno;
poststr += "&firstocc=10";
poststr += "&selfdelete=";
poststr += (selfdelete ? "1" : "0");
poststr += "&audiofile=" + filename;
// Send Call Request
String rcstr = PostToGateway(urlstr, poststr);
return GetRequestID(rcstr);
}
/// <param name="reqID">Call request ID</param>
/// <returns>status code</returns>
Public string CallStatus(string
reqID)
{
// call status url
string urlstr = "/ocall/callstatusHandler.jsp";
string poststr = "reqid=" + reqID;
// Send Call Request
```

```
String rcstr = PostToGateway(urlstr, poststr);
if (rcstr.IndexOf("^made^") != -1)
return "Call Made";
if (rcstr.IndexOf("^failed^") != -1)
return "Call Failed";
if (rcstr.IndexOf("^retry^") != -1)
return "Call Will Retry";
return "";
}
public void CallRemove(string
reqID)
{
// call status url
string urlstr = "/ocall/callremoveHandler.jsp";
string poststr = "reqid=" + reqID;
// Send Call Request
PostToGateway(urlstr, poststr);
}
```

VOICE XML:

- Voice XML is an XML based mark-up language for creating distributed voice applications.
- Voice XML supports dialogue that feature:

i. Spoken input
ii. DTMF input
iii. Recording of speech input
iv. Synthesized speech output
v. Recorded audio output
vi. Dialog flow control
vii. Scoping of input

Architectural Model

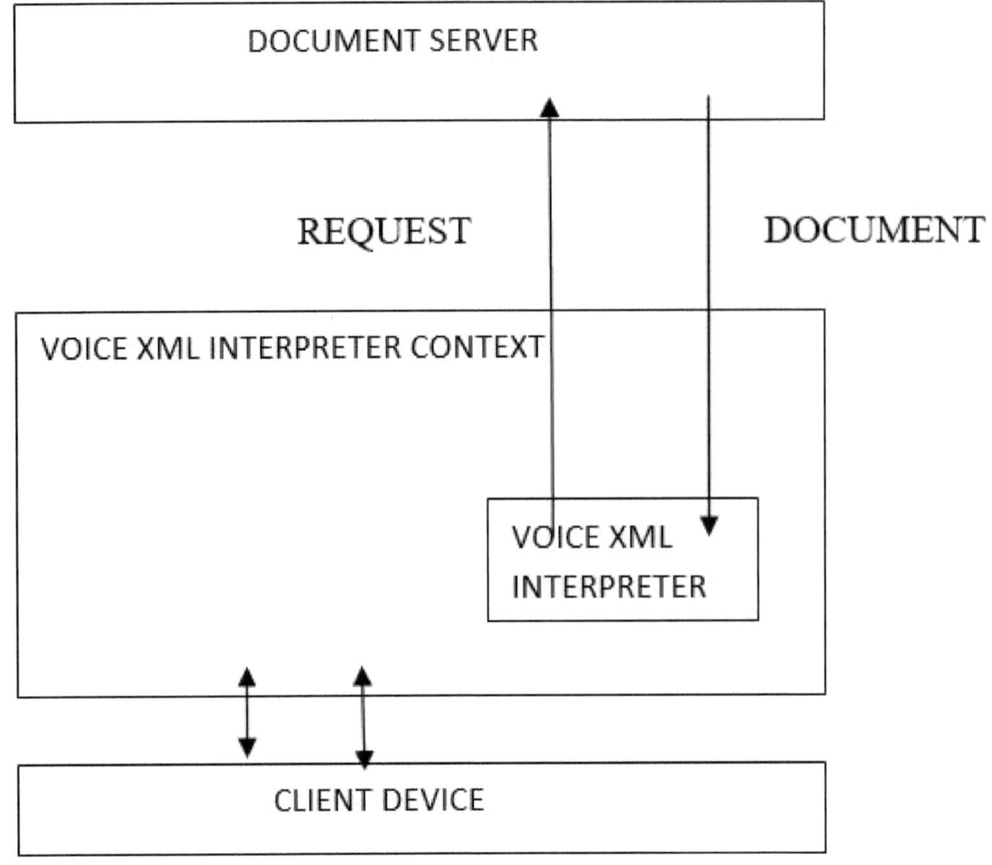

Voice Browser:

- An audio browser is similar to a virtual web browser like nets cape communication or internet explorer.
- Using voice browser, we can interact with a web server using our voice and telephone.

Dialogs:

- A voice XML application defines a series of dialogs between user and computer.
- Two types of dialogs are,

1. Forms-it collects the value for a set of fields.
2. Menus-presents the user with choice or options and then transition to another dialog based on choice

Example:

```
<? XML version= "1.0">
<VXML version = "1.0">
</VXML>
```

Prompts:

- It is used to speak the given text inside the tag.

- The prompts can either be pre recorded audio or can be synthesized speech(TTS).
- Any text within athe bdy of a <prompt> element is spoken.

Example:
<Prompt> have a nice day </Prompt>
Grammar:

- **In** voice XML we use <grammar> element to define what the caller can say to the application at any given time.

<Grammar> </Grammar>

- There are three different types of grammars:

1. Inline
2. External
3. Built-in

Inline -it is defined right in the XML code
Example: <Grammar> credit card | tuition </Grammar>
External-it is specified outside of the XML document, the reference is with in the voiceXML code.
<Grammar> src="names.Gram" type="application/x-jsgf" </Grammar>
Form:

- **It** is basically a collection of one or more fields that the caller fills by saying something.
- It is a one of the way to developing a dialog with the caller in voice XML.
- <form>àdefine the form.
- <field>àa fields within the form.

Example:
```
<? Xml version="1.0"?>
<form id ="add_funds">
<field name = "amount" type="currency">
<Prompt> how much?</prompt>
</field>
</form>
</vxml>
```
Events:
Events are thrown by the platform under various circumstances, such as

1. User does not respond
2. Requests help.
3. Does not respond intelligibly

Links:
A link <link>used to throw an event to go to a destination URI.
Voice XML elements:

1. **<Assign>**-assign a value of a variable.

2. **<Catch>**- catch an event.
3. **<Choice>**-define a menu item.
4. **<Disconnect>**-disconnect a session.
5. **<Exit>**-exit a session.
6. **<Throw>**-throw an event.
7. **<Help>**-catch a help event.
8. **<If>**-simple conditional logic.
9. **<Var>**-declare a variable.
10. **<Else>**-used in < if> element.

TAPI (TELEPHONY APPLICATION PROGRAMMING INTERFACE):

- The **Telephony Application Programming Interface (TAPI)** is a Microsoft Windows API, which provides computer telephony integration and enables PCs running Microsoft Windows to use telephone services.
- Different versions of TAPI are available on different versions of Windows. TAPI allows applications to control telephony functions between a computer and telephone network for data, fax, and voice calls.
- It includes basic functions, such as dialing, answering, and hanging up a call.
- It also supports supplementary functions, such as hold, transfer, conference, and Call Park found in PBX, ISDN, and other telephone systems.
- TAPI is used primarily to control either modems or, more recently, to control business telephone system (PBX) handsets.
- When controlling a PBX handset, the driver is provided by the manufacturer of the telephone system.
- Some manufacturers provide drivers that allow the control of multiple handsets. This is traditionally called "third-party control".
- Other manufacturers provide drivers that allow the control of a single handset. This is called "first-party control".
- Third-party drivers are designed to allow applications to see and/or control multiple extensions at the same time. Some telephone systems only permit one third-party connection at a time.
- First-party drivers are designed to allow applications to monitor and/or control one extension at a time.
- Telephone systems naturally permit many of these connections simultaneously. Modem connections are by nature first-party.
- TAPI can also be used to control voice-enabled telephony devices, including voice modems and dedicated hardware such as Dialogic cards.

CHAPTER III

EMERGING TECHNOLOGIES

BLUETOOTH

- Bluetooth is an open wireless technology standard for exchanging data over short distances (using short wavelength radio transmissions) from fixed and mobile devices, creating personal area networks (PANs) with high levels of security.
- Created by telecoms vendor Ericsson in 1994, it was originally conceived as a wireless alternative to RS-232 data cables. It can connect several devices, overcoming problems of synchronization. Today Bluetooth is managed by the Bluetooth Special Interest Group.

BLUETOOTH PROTOCOL:

- Bluetooth protocol uses the concept of master and slave.
- Several Bluetooth devices can form an ad hoc network called a "piconet"
    - In a piconet one device acts as a master (sets frequency hopping behavior) and the others as slaves
    - Example: A conference room with many laptops wishing to communicate with each other
- Pico net
    - Each piconet has one master and up to 7 simultaneous slaves
        - Master: device that initiates a data exchange.
        - Slave: device that responds to the master.
        - All devices in a piconet hop together
        - Master gives slaves its clock and device ID
        - Non-piconet devices are in standby

M=Master P=Parked
S=Slave SB=Standby

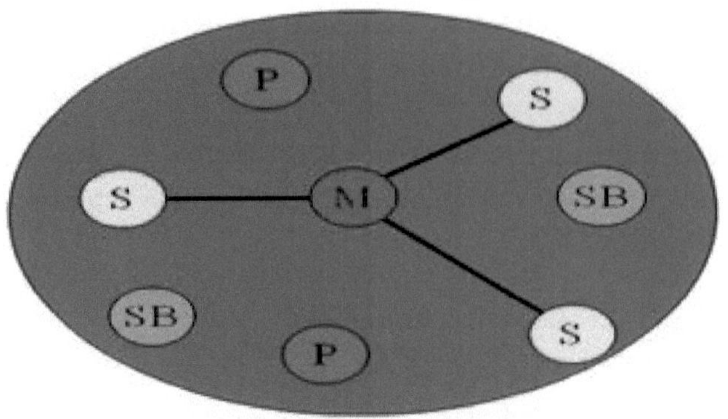

- Scatternet
    - Linking of multiple piconets through the master or slave devices

àBluetooth devices have point-to-multipoint capability to engage in Scatternet communication.Devices can be slave in one piconet and master of another

BLUETOOTH PROTOCOL STACK:

- **Bluetooth Radio :**specifics details of the air interface, including frequency, frequency hopping, modulation scheme, and transmission power.
- **Baseband:** concerned with connection establishment within a piconet, addressing, packet format, timing and power control

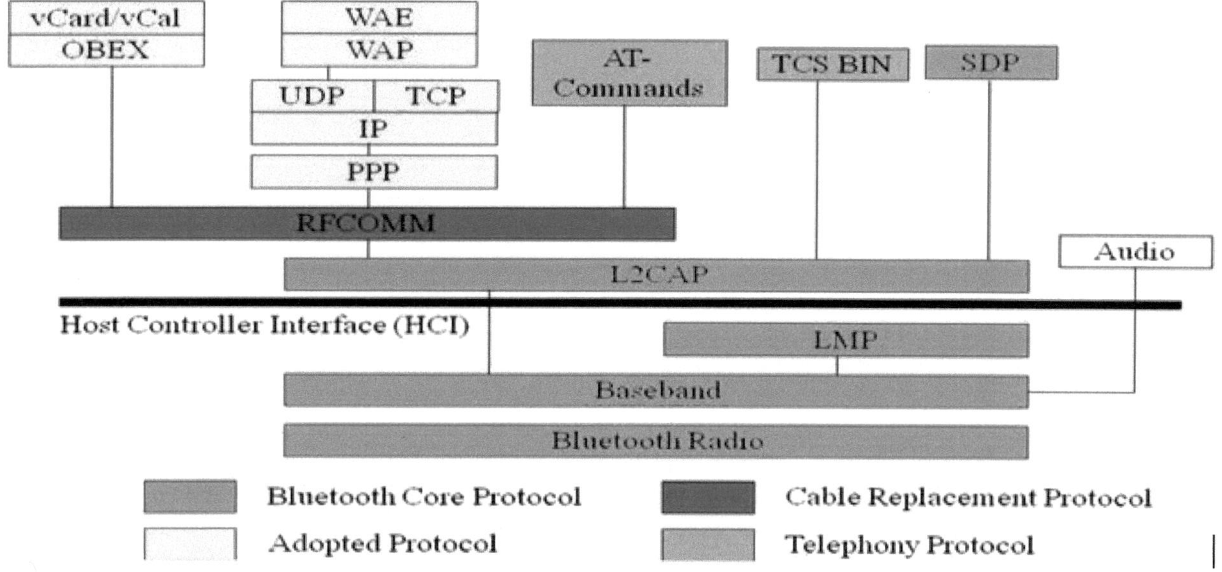

Fig: Bluetooth protocol stack

- **Link manager protocol (LMP):** establishes the link setup between Bluetooth devices and manages ongoing links, including security aspects (e.g. authentication and encryption), and control and negotiation of baseband packet size
- **Logical link control and adaptation protocol (L2CAP):** adapts upper layer protocols to the baseband layer. Provides both connectionless and connection-oriented services.
- **Service discovery protocol (SDP):** handles device information, services, and queries for service characteristics between two or more Bluetooth devices.
- **Host Controller Interface (HCI):** provides an interface method for accessing the Bluetooth hardware capabilities. It contains a command interface, which acts between the Baseband controller and link manager.
- **TCS BIN (Telephony Control Service):** bit-oriented protocol that defines the call control signaling for the establishment of voice and data calls between Bluetooth devices.
- **OBEX(OBject EXchange)** : Session-layer protocol for the exchange of objects, providing a model for object and operation representation
- **RFCOMM:** a reliable transport protocol, which provides emulation of RS232 serial ports over the L2CAP protocol
- **WAE/WAP:** Bluetooth incorporates the wireless application environment and the wireless application protocol into its architecture.

BLUETOOTH SECURITY:

- There are three modes of security for Bluetooth access between two devices.
  - non-secure
  - service level enforced security
  - link level enforced security

- Device security level
    - Trusted
    - untrusted
- Service security level
    - Authorization and Authentication
    - Authentication only
    - Open to all devices
- The following are the three basic security services specified in the Bluetooth standard:
    - **Authentication**
        - Verifying the identity of communicating devices. User authentication is not provided natively by Bluetooth.
    - **Confidentiality**
        - Preventing information compromise caused by eavesdropping by ensuring that only authorized devices can access and view data.
    - **Authorization**
        - Allowing the control of resources by ensuring that a device is authorized to use a service before permitting it to do so.

BLUETOOTH APPLICATIONS MODELS:

- Automatic synchronization between mobile and stationary devices
- Connecting mobile users to the internet using bluetooth-enabled wire-bound connection ports
- Dynamic creation of private networks
- Data and voice access points.
- Real-time voice and data transmissions
- Cable replacement
- Eliminates need for numerous cable attachments for connection
- Ad hoc networking
- Device with Bluetooth radio can establish connection with another when in range

RFID:

- RFID: RADIO FREQUENCY IDENTIFICATION
- What is RFID? Radio-frequency identification (RFID) is an automatic identification method using radio waves. RFID also began to see use in wildlife monitoring and research. RFID tags can be used to monitor animal movement without adversely affecting the animal,
- There's a chip
- Implanted RFID tags in Humans

- Applications: Supply chain automation Asset tracking Medical applications People tracking Manufacturing Retail Warehouses Livestock Timing
- The RFID System Tag. Reader. Reader antenna. Controller. Host and software system. Communication infrastructure.
- Tag An RFID tag is a device that can store and transmit data to a reader in a contact less manner using radio waves. RFID tags can be classified in three different ways.

  1. Passive tags
  2. Active tags

- Passive Tag No on-board power source (for example, a battery) Uses the power emitted from the reader to energize itself and transmit its stored data to the reader always communicates first, followed by the tag.
- Smaller than an active or semi-active tag. It has a variety of read ranges starting with less than 1 inch to about 30 feet (9 meters approximately). Cheaper compared to an active or semi-active tag.
- Active Tag has on-board power source (for example, a battery; other sources of power, such as solar, are also possible) Own on-board power supply to transmit its data to a reader. No need for reader's emitted power for data transmission.
- A tag always communicates first, followed by the reader. Can broadcast its data to its surroundings even in the absence of a reader
- Another way to Classify Tags Read-only (RO) Write once, read many (WORM) Read-writes (RW)
- The RFID System Tag. Reader. Reader antenna. Controller. Host and software system. Communication infrastructure.
- Advantages Contactless. An RFID tag can be read without any physical contact between the tag and the reader. Writable data. The data of a read-write (RW) RFID tag can be rewritten a large number of times. Absence of line of sight. A line of sight is generally not required for an RFID reader to read an RFID tag.
- Advantages.

1. Variety of read ranges.
2. Wide data-capacity range.
3. Support for multiple tag reads.
4. Perform smart tasks.

- Disadvantages

1. Poor performance with RF-opaque and RF-absorbent objects.
2. Impacted by environmental factors.
3. Limitation on actual tag reads.
4. Impacted by hardware interference

- CONCLUSION : RFID, is an emerging technology which can be used for a variety of applications. However, the potential for abuse of this technology is vast and requires careful consideration to avoid.
- Radio-frequency identification (RFID) is a technology that uses communication via electromagnetic waves to exchange data between a terminal and an object such as a product, animal, or person for the purpose of identification and tracking.
- Some tags can be read from several meters away and beyond the line of sight of the reader.
- Radio-frequency identification involves interrogators, and tags.
- Most RFID tags contain at least two parts. One is an integrated circuit for storing and processing information, modulating and demodulating a radio-frequency (RF) signal, and other specialized functions.

- The other is an antenna for receiving and transmitting the signal.
- There are three types of RFID tags: passive RFID tags, which have no power source and require an external electromagnetic field to initiate a signal transmission, active RFID tags, which contain a battery and can transmit signals once an external source ('Interrogator') has been successfully identified, and battery assisted passive (BAP) RFID tags, which require an external source to wake up but have significant higher forward link capability providing greater range.

Areas of applications for RFID:

- Access management
- Tracking of goods and RFID in retail
- Tracking of persons and animals
- Toll collection and contactless payment
- Machine readable travel documents
- Smart dust (for massively distributed sensor networks)
- Location-based services
- Tracking sports memorabilia to verify authenticity
- Airport baggage tracking logistics

WiMAX:
Introduction:

- WiMAX (Worldwide Interoperability for Microwave Access) is a telecommunications protocol that provides fixed and fully mobile Internet access.
- The current WiMAX revision provides up to 40 Mbit/s with the IEEE 802.16m update expected to offer up to 1 Gbit/s fixed speeds.
- Goal: Provide high-speed Internet access to home and business subscribers, without wires

- Wireless PANs (Bluetooth – IEEE 802.15)
  - very low range
  - wireless connection to printers etc
- Wireless LANs (Wi-Fi – IEEE 802.11)
  - infrastructure as well as ad-hoc networks possible
  - home/office networking
- Multi hup Ad hoc Networks
  - useful when infrastructure not available, impractical, or expensive
  - military applications, emergencies
- Wireless MANs (WiMAX-802.16)
  - Similar to cellular networks
  - Traditional base station infrastructure systems.

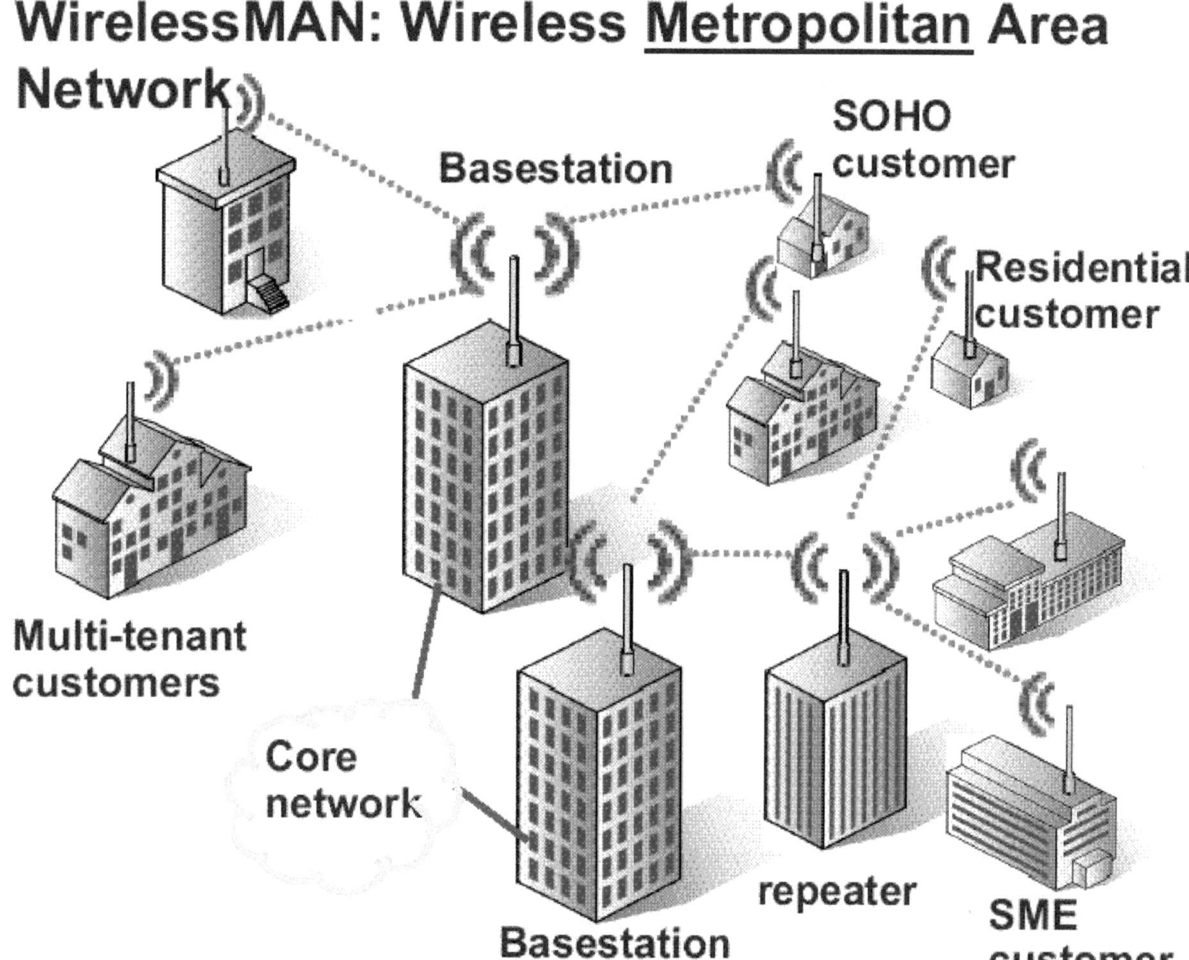

(WiMAX-802.16) standards:

1. IEEE 802.16.1- air interface for 10 to 66 GHz
2. IEEE.802.16.2- coexistence of broadband wireless access system.
3. IEEE.802.16.3- Air interface for licensed frequencies,2 to 11 GHz.

802.16 Three layer architecture:

It has three layers:

1. The physical layer
2. Media access control layer (MAC).
3. Convergence layer

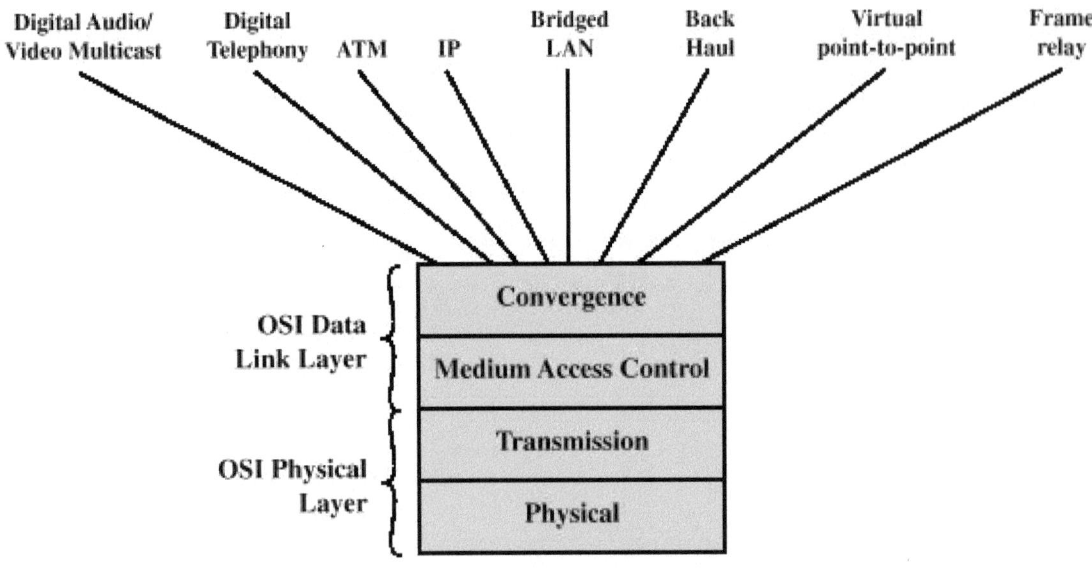

802.16 Three layer architecture

1. The physical layer:

- Allows use of directional antennas
- Allows use of two different duplexing schemes:
    - Frequency Division Duplexing (FDD)
    - Time Division Duplexing (TDD)
- Support for both full and half duplex stations
- Adaptive Data Burst profiles
    - Transmission parameters (e.g. Modulation, FEC) can be modified on a frame-by-frame basis for each SS
    - Profiles are identified by "Interval Usage Code".
- Physical layer functions:
    - Encoding/decoding of signals
    - Preamble generation/removal.

1. Medium access control layer (MAC):
    - On transmission, assemble data into a frame with address and error detection fields
    - On reception, disassemble frame, and perform address recognition and error detection
    - Govern access to the wireless transmission medium.

3. Convergence layer functions:

a. Encapsulate PDU framing of upper layers into native 802.16 MAC/PHY frames
b. Map upper layer's addresses into 802.16 addresses
c. Translate upper layer QoS parameters into native 802.16 MAC format
d. Adapt time dependencies of upper layer traffic into equivalent MAC service.

Broadband applications:
These application areas are:

- Video–based applications;
- Telehealth applications;
- Distance learning applications;
- E–government applications; and,
- Emergency management operations applications.

<u>MOBILE IP:</u>

Introduction:

- Mobile IP (or IP mobility) is an Internet Engineering Task Force (IETF) standard communications protocol that is designed to allow mobile device users to move from one network to another while maintaining a permanent IP address.
- Mobile IP for IPv4 is described in IETF RFC 3344, and updates are added in IETF RFC 4721.
- Mobile IPv6, the IP mobility implementation for the next generation of the Internet Protocol, IPv6, is described in RFC 3775.
- IP was developed as a means for transparently dealing wiMobile the problems of mobile users
    - Enables hosts to stay connected to the Internet regardless of their location
    - Enables hosts to be tracked without needing to change their IP address
    - Requires no changes to software of non-mobile hosts/routers
    - Requires addition of some infrastructure
    - Has no geographical limitations
    - Requires no modifications to IP addresses or IP address format
    - Supports security
        - Could be even more important than physically connected routing
- IETF standardization process is still underway

How does mobile IP work:

- Mobile Node (MN)
    - The entity that may change its point of attachment from network to network in the Internet
        - Detects it has moved and registers with "best" FA
    - Assigned a permanent IP called its *home address* to which other hosts send packets regardless of MN's location
        - Since this IP doesn't change it can be used by long-lived applications as MN's location changes

- Home Agent (HA)
    - This is router with additional functionality
    - Located on home network of MN
    - Does mobility binding of MN's IP with its COA
    - Forwards packets to appropriate network when MN is away.
        - Does this through encapsulation
- Foreign Agent (FA)
    - Another router with enhanced functionality
    - If MN is away from HA the it uses an FA to send/receive data to/from HA
    - Advertises itself periodically
    - Forward's MN's registration request
    - Decapsulates messages for delivery to MN.
- Care-of-address (COA)
    - Address which identifies MN's current location
    - Sent by FA to HA when MN attaches
    - Usually the IP address of the FA
- Correspondent Node (CN)
    - End host to which MN is corresponding (eg. a web server).

IP works:

- A MN listens for agent advertisement and then initiates registration
    - If responding agent is the HA, then mobile IP is not necessary
- After receiving the registration request from a MN, the HA acknowledges and registration is complete
    - Registration happens as often as MN changes networks.
- HA intercepts all packets destined for MN
    - This is simple unless sending application is on or near the same network as the MN.
    - HA masquerades as MN
    - There is a specific lifetime for service before a MN must re-register
    - There is also a de-registration process with HA if an MN returns home.
- HA then encapsulates all packets addressed to MN and forwards them to FA
    - IP tunneling

- FA decapsulates all packets addressed to MN and forwards them via hardware address (learned as part of registration process)
- NOTE that the MN can perform FA functions if it acquires an IP address e.g. via DHCP
- Bidirectional communications require tunneling in each direction

Mobile IP Support Services:

- Agent Discovery
    - HA's and FA's broadcast their presence on each network to which they are attached
        - Beacon messages via ICMP Router Discovery Protocol (IRDP)
    - MN's listen for advertisement and then initiate registration.
- Registration
    - When MN is away, it registers its COA with its HA
        - Typically through the FA with strongest signal
    - Registration control messages are sent via UDP to well known port.

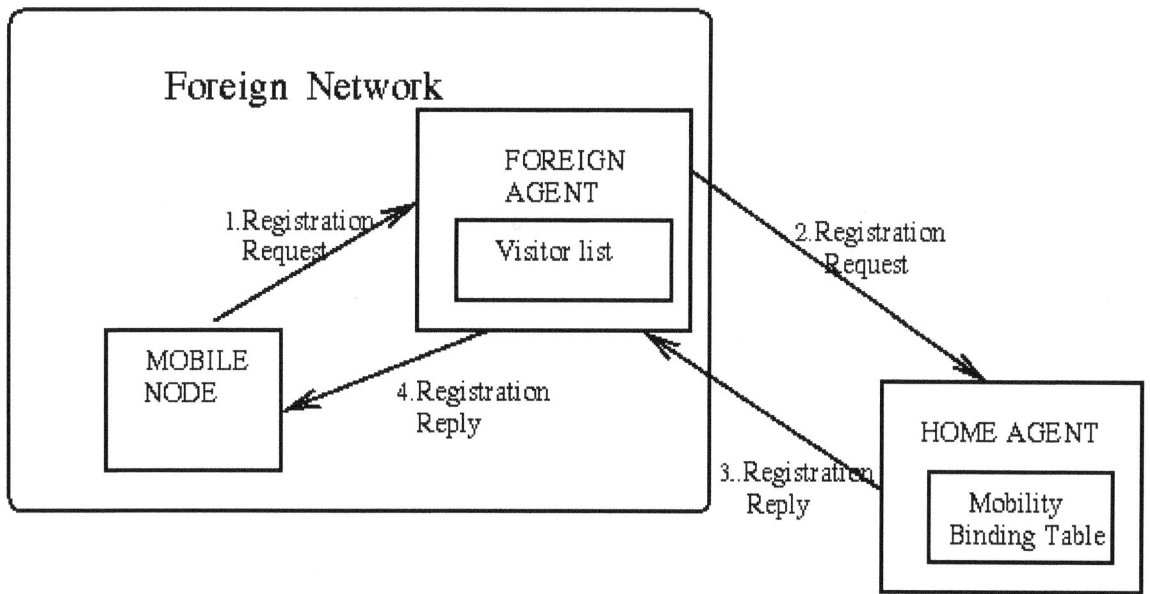

Tunneling:

- IN mobile IP, IP-within-IP encapsulation is used.
- Using IP-within-IP,the home agent, adds a new IP header called tunnel header.
- The new Tunnel header uses the mobile nodes care-of-address as the tunnel destination IP address.

- The tunnel source IP address is the Home Agents IP address.
- The tunnel header uses 4 as a protocol number àindicating the next protocol header is gain an IP header.
- The Foreign agent after receiving the packet drops the tunnel header and delivers the rest to the mobile node.
- Next, the home agent intercept all IP data datagram packet sent to the mobile node via tunneling.
- The Home Agent informs other nodes in the home network.

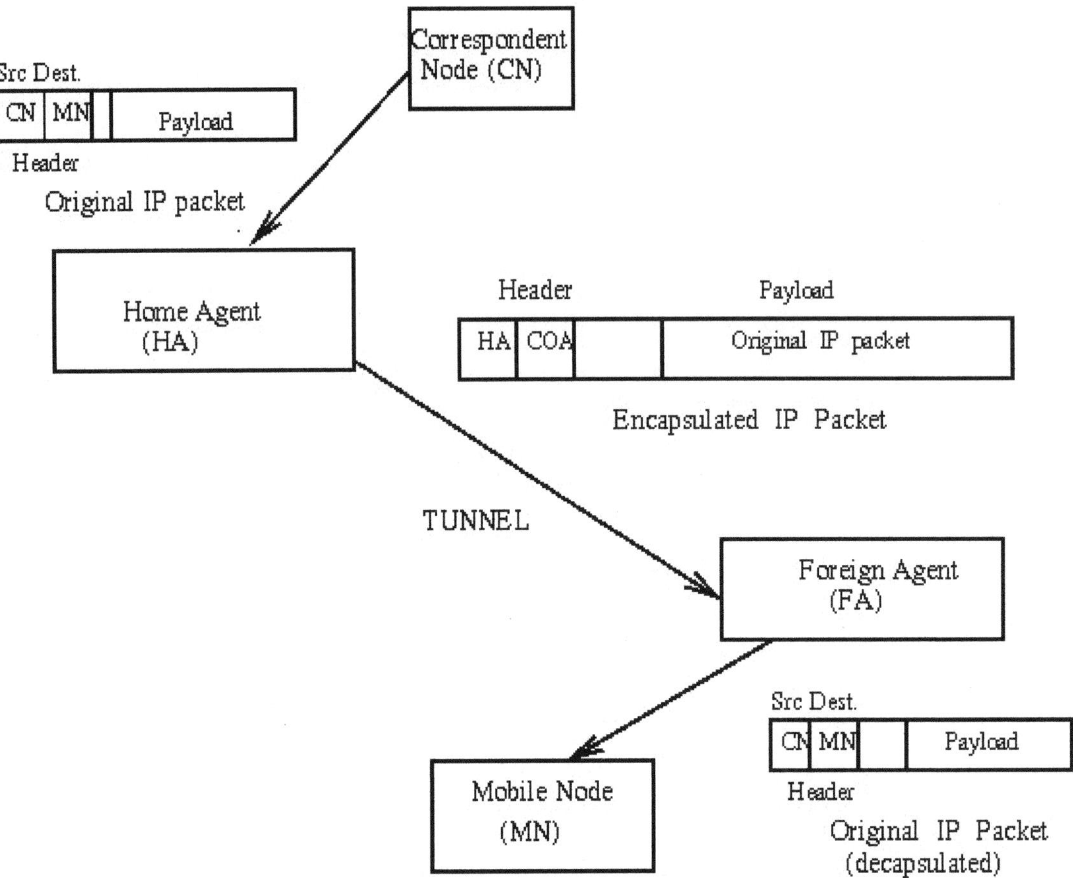

Applications

- Mobile IP is most often found in wired and wireless environments where users need to carry their mobile devices across multiple LAN subnets.
- Examples of use are in roaming between overlapping wireless systems, e.g., IP over DVB, WLAN, WiMAX and BWA. Currently, Mobile IP is not required within cellular systems such as 3G, to provide transparency when Internet users migrate between cellular towers, since these systems provide their own data link layer handover and roaming mechanisms.
- However, it is often used in 3G systems to allow seamless IP mobility between different Packet Data Serving Node (PDSN) domains.

INTERNET PROTOCOL VERSION 6 (IPV6):

- Internet Protocol Version 6 (IPv6) is a version of the Internet Protocol that is designed to succeed Internet Protocol version 4 (IPv4), the first publicly used Internet Protocol in operation since 1981.
- IPv6 is an Internet Layer protocol for packet-switched internetworking. The main driving force for the redesign of Internet Protocol was the foreseeable IPv4 address exhaustion.
- IPv6 was developed by the Internet Engineering Task Force (IETF), and is described in Internet standard document RFC 2460, published in December 1998.
- 128-bit address space
- This is what it's all about...
- Real-time/Quos services
- Security and authentication
- Auto configuration
- Hosts autoconfig with IP address and domain name
- Idea is to try to make systems more plug-n-play
- Enhanced routing functionality e.g. Mobile hosts
- Multicast
- Protocol extensions
- Smooth transition path from IPv4

Address space:

- Allocation is classless
    - Prefixes specify different uses (unicast, multicast, anycast)
        - Anycast: send packets to nearest member of a group
    - Prefixes can be used to map v4 to v6 space and visa-versa
    - Lots of flexibility with 128 bits!
        - ~1500 address/sqft of the earths surface
- Standard representation is set of eight 16-bit values separated by colons
    - E.g. 47CD:1234:3200:0000:0000:4325:B792:0428
    - If there are large number of zeros, they can be omitted with series of colons
        - E.g. 47CD:1234:3200::4325:B792:0428
    - Address prefixes (slash notation) are the same as v4
        - E.g. FEDC:BA98:7600::/40 describes a 40 bit prefix

IPv6 security:

- IPSec standards apply to both IPv4 and IPv6
- All implementations required to support authentication and encryption headers ("IPSec")
- Authentication separate from encryption for use
  in situations where encryption is prohibited or prohibitively expensive

- Key distribution protocols are not yet defined (independent of IP v4/v6)
- Support for manual key configuration required

Packet payload:

- The IPv6 packet is shown in Figure 27.1. Each packet is composed of a mandatory base header followed by the payload.
- The payload consists of two parts: optional extension headers and data from an upper layer. The base header occupies 40 bytes, whereas the extension headers and data from the upper layer contain up to 65,535 bytes of information.

Migrating from IPv4 to IPV6:

- There is no change in physical layers between ipv4 and ipv6.
- IP tunneling IPv6 packets can propagate over an IPv4 envelope.
- Migration of computing nodes in the network: this will need the operating system upgrades so that they support IPv6 along with IPv4.
- Migration of networking applications in both client and server systems: it requites porting of applications from IPv4 to Ipv6 environment.

Mobile IP with IPv6:

- A set of mobility options to include in mobility messages
- A new Home Address option for the Destination Options header
- A new Type 2 Routing header
- New Internet Control Message Protocol for IPv6 (ICMPv6) messages to discover the set of home agents and to obtain the prefix of the home link
- Changes to router discovery messages and options and additional Neighbor Discovery options
- Foreign Agents are no longer needed

JAVA CARD:
INTRODUCTION:

- Java Card refers to a technology that allows Java-based applications (applets) to be run securely on smart cards and similar small memory footprint devices.
- Java Card is the tiniest of Java targeted for embedded devices. Java Card gives the user ability to program the device and make them application specific.
- It is widely used in SIM cards (used in GSM mobile phones) and ATM cards.
- The first Java Card was introduced in 1996 by Schlumberger's card division which later merged with Gem plus to form Gemalto.
- Java Card products are based on the Java Card Platform specifications developed by Sun Microsystems, a subsidiary of Oracle Corporation.
- Many Java card products also rely on the Global Platform specifications for the secure management of applications on the card (download, installation, personalization, deletion).
- The main design goals of the Java Card technology are portability and security.

Security

- Java Card technology was originally developed for the purpose of securing sensitive information stored on smart cards.
- Security is determined by various aspects of this technology:

Data encapsulation.

- Data is stored within the application, and Java Card applications are executed in an isolated environment (the Java Card VM), separate from the underlying operating system and hardware.

Applet Firewall.

- Unlike other Java VMs, a Java Card VM usually manages several applications, each one controlling sensitive data. Different applications are therefore separated from each other by an applet firewall which restricts and checks access of data elements of one applet to another.

Cryptography.

- Commonly used encryption algorithms like DES, Triple DES, AES, RSA (including elliptic curve cryptography) are supported. Other cryptographic services like signing, key generation and key exchange are also supported.

Applet.

- The applet is a state machine which processes only incoming command requests and responds by sending data or response status words back to the interface device.

GSM[GLOBAL SYSTEM FOR MOBILE COOMUNICATION]:

- GSM (Global System for Mobile Communications: originally from (Group Special Mobile) is the most popular standard for mobile telephony systems in the world.
- GSM differs from its predecessor technologies in that both signaling and speech channels are digital, and thus GSM is considered a second generation (2G) mobile phone system.
- This also facilitates the wide-spread implementation of data communication applications into the system.
- The GSM standard has been an advantage to both consumers, who may benefit from the ability to roam and switch carriers without replacing phones, and also to network operators, who can choose equipment from many GSM equipment vendors.
- GSM also pioneered low-cost implementation of the short message service (SMS), also called text messaging, which has since been supported on other mobile phone standards as well.

GSM ARCHITECTURE:

INTRODUCTION:

The structure of a GSM network .The network is structured into a number of discrete sections:

- The Base Station Subsystem (the base stations and their controllers).
- The Network and Switching Subsystem (the part of the network most similar to a fixed network). This is sometimes also just called the core network.
- The GPRS Core Network (the optional part which allows packet based Internet connections).

- The Operations support system (OSS) for maintenance of the network.

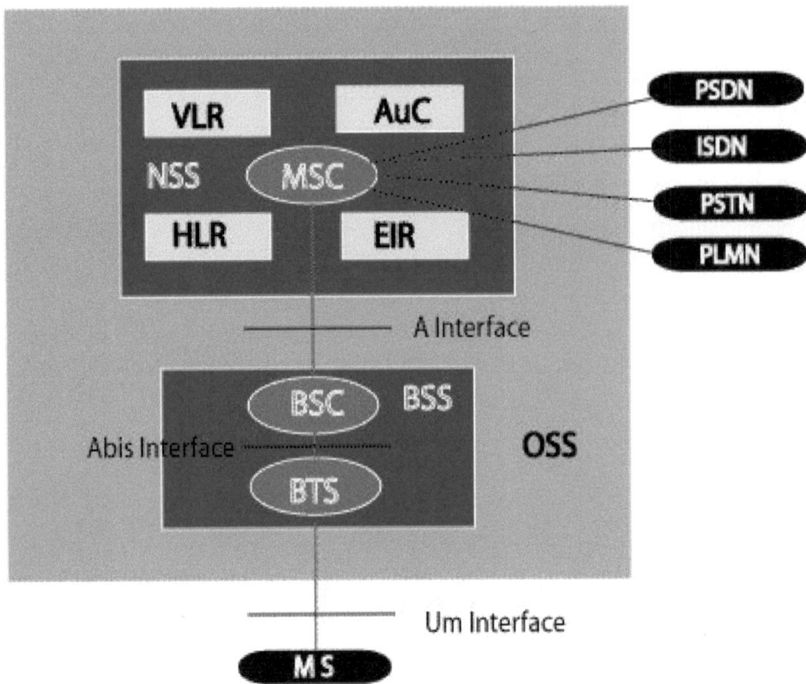

Architecture of GSM Network

The added components of the GSM architecture include the functions of the databases and messaging systems:

- Home Location Register (HLR)
- Visitor Location Register (VLR)
- Equipment Identity Register (EIR)
- Authentication Centre (AuC)
- SMS Serving Centre SMS SC)
- Gateway MSC (GMSC)
- Chargeback Centre (CBC)
- Transcoder and Adaptation Unit (TRAU)

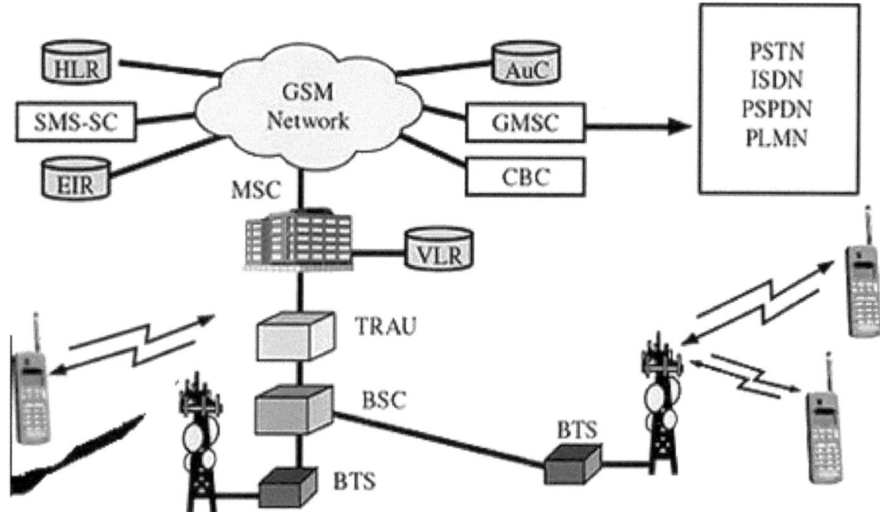

GSM Network

- The MS and the BSS communicate across the Um interface, also known as the air interface or radio link.
- The BSS communicates with the Network Service Switching center across the A interface.

GSM network areas:

In a GSM network, the following areas are defined:

- **Cell:** Cell is the basic service area: one BTS covers one cell. Each cell is given a Cell Global Identity (CGI), a number that uniquely identifies the cell.
- **Location Area:** A group of cells form a Location Area. This is the area that is paged when a subscriber gets an incoming call. Each Location Area is assigned a Location Area Identity (LAI). Each Location Area is served by one or more BSCs.
- **MSC/VLR Service Area:** The area covered by one MSC is called the MSC/VLR service area.
- **PLMN:** The area covered by one network operator is called PLMN. A PLMN can contain one or more MSCs.

GSM ENTITIES:
The network is divided into four main groups:

- The Mobile Station (MS). -->it includes the Mobile Equipment and the Subscriber Identity Module [SIM].
- The Base Station Subsystem (BSS).
- The Network and Switching Subsystem (NSS).
- The Operation and Support Subsystem (OSS).

1. A Mobile Station consists of two main elements:

- **The Subscriber Identity Module (SIM):** It is protected by a four-digit Personal Identification Number (PIN). In order to identify the subscriber to the system, the SIM card contains amongst others a unique International Mobile Subscriber I density (IMSI). User mobility is provided through mapping the subscriber to the SIM card rather than the terminal as we done in past cellular systems.

- **Mobile equipment/terminal (ME):** There are different types of terminals (MN) distinguished principally by their power and application:

  - `Fixed' terminals mainly installed in cars. Their maximum allowed output power is **20W**

  - Portable terminals can also be installed in vehicles. Their maximum allowed output power is **8W**.
  - Handheld terminals; their popularity is owed to their weight and volume, which is continuously decreasing. According to some specification these terminals may emit up to **0.8W**. However, as technology has evolved their maximum allowed power output is limited to **0.1W**

2. Base Station Subsystem

The BSS provides the interface between the ME and the NSS. It is in charge of the transmission and reception. It may be divided into two parts:

- **Base Station Controller (BSC):** It controls a group of BTSs and manages their radio resources. A BSC is principally **in charge ofhandoffs**, frequency hopping, *exchange* functions and ***power control*** over each managed BTSs.
- **Base Transceiver Station (BTS) or Base Station:** it maps to transceivers and antennas used in **each cell** of the network. It is usually placed in the center of a cell. **Its transmitting power defines the size of a cell.** Each BTS has between 1-16 transceivers depending on the density of users in the center.

3.The Network and Switching Subsystem (NSS):

Its main role is to manage the communications between the mobile users and other users, such as mobile users, ISDN users, fixed telephony users, etc. It also includes data bases needed in order to store information about the subscribers and to manage their mobility. The different components of the NSS are described below.

- **MSC:** the central component of the NSS. The MSC performs the switching functions of the network. It also provides connection to other networks.
- **GMSC:** A gateway that interconnects two networks: the **cellular network** and the **PSTN**. It is in charge of routing calls from the fixed network towards a GSM user..
- **HLR:** The HLR stores information of the suscribers belonging to the coverage area of a MSC; it also stores the current location of these subscribers and the services to which they have access. .
- **VLR:** contains information from a subscriber's HLR necessary to provide the subscribed services to visiting users. When a subscriber enters the covering area of a new MSC, the VLR associated to this MSC will request information about the new subscriber to its corresponding HLR.
- **Authentication Center (AuC):** It serves security purposes; it provides the parameters needed for authentication and encryption functions. These parameters allow verification of the subscriber's identity.
- **Equipment Identity Register (EIR):** EIR stores security-sensitive information about the mobile equipments. It maintains a list of all valid terminals as identified by their International Mobile Equipment Identity (IMEI).
- **GSM Interworking Unit (GIWU):** The GIWU provides an interface to various networks for data communications. During these communications, the transmission of speech and data can be alternated.

4. Operation and Support Subsystem (OSS)

- It is connected to components of the NSS and the BSC, in order to **control and monitor** the GSM system.
- It is also in charge of controlling the **traffic load** of the BSS.
- It must be noted that as the number of BS *increases* with the scaling of the subscriber population some of the maintenance tasks are transferred to the BTS, allowing *savings* in the cost of ownership of the system.

<u>CALL ROUTING IN GSM:</u>

The two types of routings are:

- Call Originating from MS.
- Call termination to MS.

Call Originating from MS

1. MS sends dialed number to BSS
2. BSS sends dialed number to MSC
3. MSC checks VLR if MS is allowed the requested service.
4. If so, MSC asks BSS to allocate resources for call.

5. MSC routes the call to GMSC
6. GMSC routes the call to local exchange of called user
7. 7, 8,
8. 9,10 Answer back(ring back) tone is routed from called user to MS via GMSC,MSC,BSS

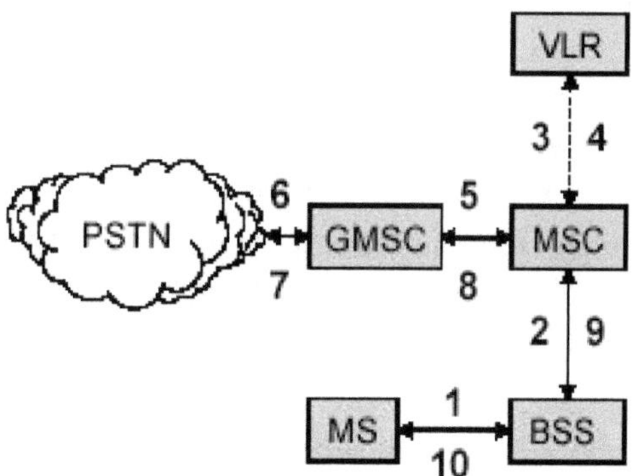

<u>Call termination to MS.</u>

1. Calling a GSM subscribers
2. Forwarding call to GSMC
3. Signal Setup to HLR
4. 5. Request MSRN from VLR
5. Forward responsible MSC to GMSC
6. Forward Call to current MSC
7. 9. Get current status of MS
8. 11. Paging of MS

9. 13. MS answers
10. 15. Security checks
11. 17. Set up connection

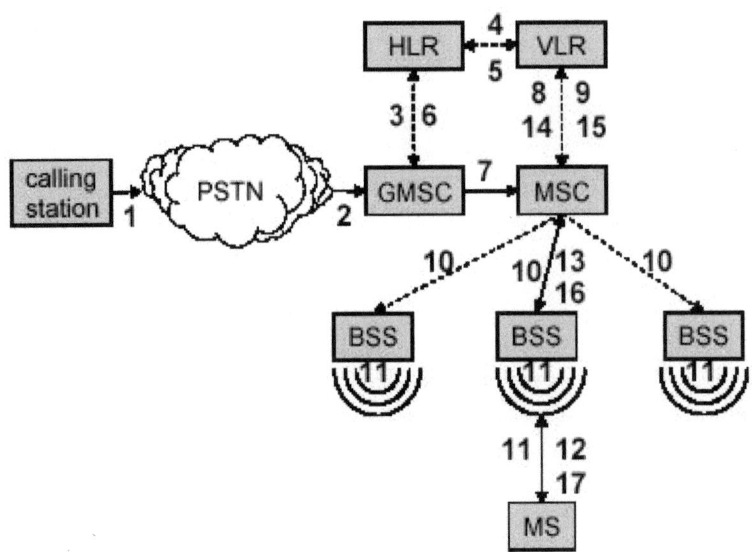

PLMN INTERFACES:

- A public land mobile network (PLMN) is any wireless communications system intended for use by terrestrial subscribers in vehicles or on foot.
- Such a system can stand alone, but often it is interconnected with a fixed system such as the PSTN.
- The most familiar example of a PLMN end user is a person with a cell phone.
- However, mobile and portable Internet use is also becoming common.
- The general objective of a PLMN is to facilitate wireless communication and to interlink the wireless network with the fixed wired network.
- The PLMN was specified by the European Telecommunications Standard Institute (ETSI) following up with their GSM specification.
- To give access to the GSM network for a mobile subscriber in a country that operates the GSM system.
- To provide facilities for automatic roaming, locating and updating of mobile subscribers.
- To provide the subscriber a wide range of services and facilities.
- Both voice and non voice that are compatible with those offered by existing networks like PSTN and ISDN.
- GSM network contains central HLR and a central VLR.

HLR-contains all security, provisioning and subscriber related information.

2. VLR -stores the location information and other transient data.
3. MSC -needs subscriber parameter for successful call set-up.

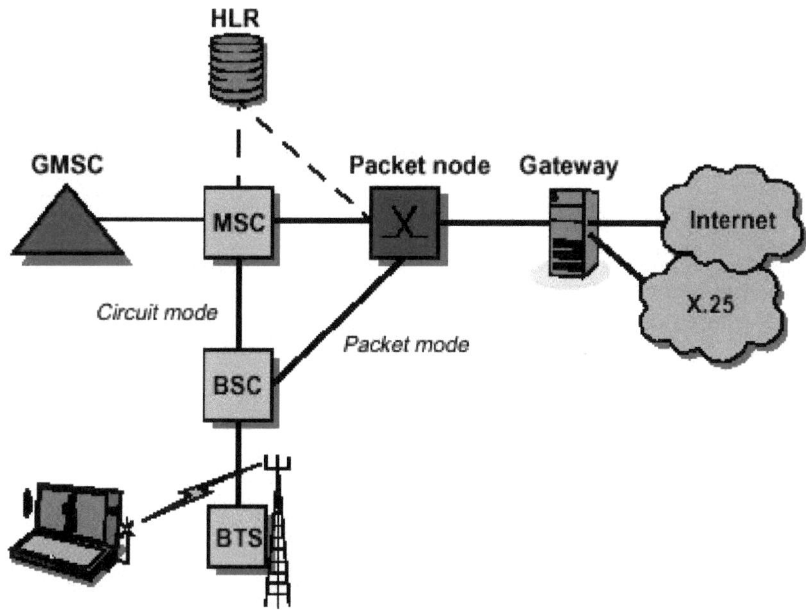

<u>GSM ADDRESSES AND IDENTIFIERS</u>:

The most important addresses and identifiers are presented in the following:

1. International Mobile Station Equipment Identity (IMEI):

- The international mobile station equipment identity (IMEI) uniquely identifies a mobile station internationally.
- It is a kind of serial number. The IMEI is allocated by the equipment manufacturer and registered by the network operator and registered by the network operator who stores it in the EIR.There are following parts of an IMEI:

- **Type Approval Code (TAC):** 6 decimal places, centrally assigned.
- **Final Assembly Code (FAC):** 6 decimal places, assigned by the manufacturer.
- **Serial Number (SNR):** 6 decimal places, assigned by the manufacturer.
- **Spare (SP):** 1 decimal place.

Thus, IMEI = TAC + FAC + SNR + SP. It uniquely characterizes a mobile station and gives clues about the manufacturer and the date of manufacturing.

2. International Mobile Subscriber Identity (IMSI):

Each registered user is uniquely identified by its international mobile subscriber identity (IMSI). It is stored in the subscriber identity module (SIM) A mobile station can only be operated if a SIM with a valid IMSI is inserted into equipment with a valid IMEI.

There are following parts of an IMSI:

- **Mobile Country Code (MCC):** 3 decimal places, internationally standardized.
- **Mobile Network Code (MNC):** 2 decimal places, for unique identification of mobile network within the country.
- **Mobile Subscriber Identification Number (MSIN):** Maximum 10 decimal places, identification number of the subscriber in the home mobile network.

3. *Mobile Subscriber ISDN Number (MSISDN):*

- The *real telephone number* of a mobile station is the mobile subscriber ISDN number (MSISDN).
- It is assigned to the subscriber (his or her SIM, respectively), such that a mobile station set can have several MSISDNs depending on the SIM.

The MSISDN categories follow the international ISDN number plan and therefore have the following structure.

- **Country Code (CC):** Up to 3 decimal places.
- **National Destination Code (NDC):** Typically 2-3 decimal places.
- **Subscriber Number (SN):** Maximum 10 decimal places.

4. *Mobile Station Roaming Number (MSRN):*

- The Mobile Station Roaming Number (MSRN) is a temporary location dependent ISDN number.
- It is assigned by the locally responsible VLR to each mobile station in its area. Calls are also routed to the MS by using the MSRN.

The MSRN has same structure as the MSISDN.

- **Country Code (CC):** of the visited network.
- **National Destination Code (NDC):** of the visited network.
- **Subscriber Number (SN):** in the current mobile network.

5. *Location Area Identity (LAI):*

- Each LA of a PLMN has its own identifier.
- The Location Area Identifier (LAI) is also structured hierarchically and internationally unique as follows:

- **Country Code (CC) :** 3 decimal places.
- **Mobile Network Code (MNC):** 2 decimal places.
- **Location Area Code (LAC):** maximum 5 decimal places or, maximum twice 8 bits coded in hexadecimal (LAC < FFFF).

6. *Temporary Mobile Subscriber Identity (TMSI):*

- The VLR, which is responsible for the current location of a subscriber, can assign a temporary mobile subscriber identity (TMSI) which has only local significance in the area handled by the VLR.
- It is stored on the network side only in the VLR and is not passed to the HLR.

- Together with the current location area, TMSI allows a subscriber to be identified uniquely and it can consist of upto 4x8 bits.

7. Local Mobile Subscriber Identity (LMSI):

- The VLR can assign an additional searching key to each mobile station within its area to accelerate database access.
- This unique key is called the Local Mobile Subscriber Identity (LMSI).
- The LMSI is assigned when the mobile station registers with the VLR and is also sent to the HLR.
- An LIMSI consists of four octets (4 x 8 bits).

8. Cell Identifier (CI):

Within an LA, the individual cells are uniquely identified with a cell identifier (CI), maximum 2 x 8 bits. Together with the global cell identity (LAI + CI) calls are thus also internationally defined in a unique way.

<u>NETWORK ASPECTS IN GSM</u>

- The layered model of the GSM architecture integrates and links the peer-to-peer communications between two different systems.
- The underlying layers satisfy the services of the upper-layer protocols.
- Notifications are passed from layer to layer to ensure that the information has been properly formatted, transmitted, and received.

The GMS protocol stacks diagram is shown below:

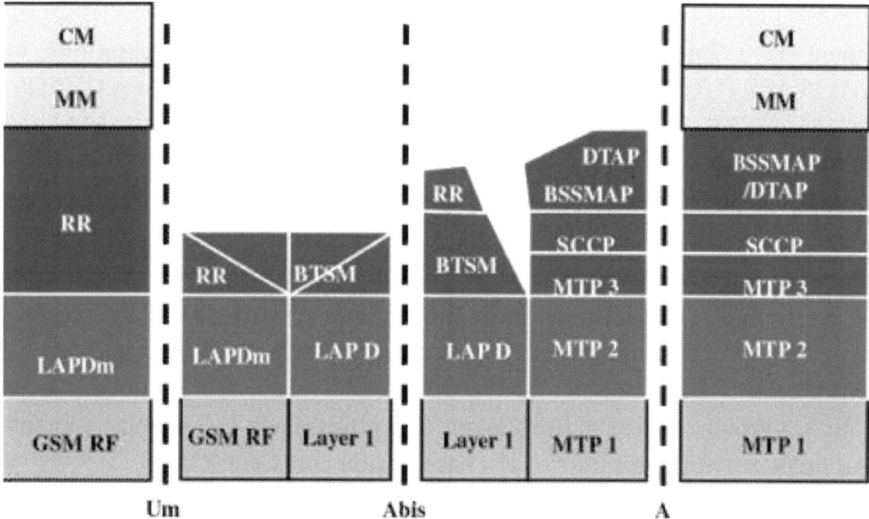

MS Protocols:

The signaling protocol in GSM is structured into three general layers, depending on the interface.

- **Layer 1:** The physical layer, which uses the channel structures over the air interface.

- **Layer 2:** The data-link layer. Across the Um interface, the data-link layer is a modified version of the Link access protocol for the D channel (LAP-D) protocol used in ISDN, called Link access protocol on the Dm channel (LAP-Dm). Across the A interface, the Message Transfer Part (MTP), Layer 2 of SS7 is used.
- **Layer 3:** The third layer of the GSM signaling protocol is divided into three sub layers:

    - Radio Resource management (RR)àcontrols the set-up, maintenance, and termination of radio and fixed channels, including handovers.
    - Mobility Management (MM) àmanages the location, updating the registration procedures as well as security and authentication.
    - Connection Management (CM) --> handles general call control.

1. Handover

- The term **handover** or **handoff** refers to the process of transferring an ongoing call or data session from one channel connected to the core network to another.
- This procedure is called Handoff in North America.

There are four types of handover in GSM system, which involves transferring a call between:

1. Channels in the same cell.
2. Cells under the control of the same Base Station Controller (BSC).
3. Cells under the control of different BSC belonging to same MSC.
4. Cells under the control of MSC.

- The 1st two types of handovers are internal handovers involves only one Base Station Controller (BSC).
- The last two types of handover called external handover—are handled by MSC.

2. Mobility management:

- Mobility management is a functionality that facilitates mobile device operations in Universal Mobile Telecommunications System (UMTS) or Global System for Mobile Communications (GSM) networks.
- Mobility management is used to trace physical user and subscriber locations to provide mobile phone services, like calls and Short Message Service (SMS).
- UMTS and GSM are each made up of separate cells (base stations) that cover a specific geographical area.

- The location update procedure allows a mobile device to notify a cellular network when shifting between areas.
- When a mobile device recognizes that an area code differs from a previous update, the mobile device executes a location update, by sending a location request to its network, prior location and specific Temporary Mobile Subscriber Identity (TMSI).
- Location area includes a group of base stations assembled collectively to optimize signaling. Base stations are integrated to form a single network area known as a base station controller (BSC).
- The BSC manages allocation of radio channels, acquires measurements from cell phones, and handles handovers from one base station to another.

Roaming

- Roaming is one of the fundamental mobility management procedures of all cellular networks.
- Roaming is defined as the ability for a cellular customer to automatically make and receive voice calls, send and receive data, or access other services, including home data services, when travelling outside the geographical coverage area of the home network, by means of using a visited network.
- This can be done by using a communication terminal or else just by using the subscriber identity in the visited network.
- Roaming is technically supported by mobility management, authentication, authorization and billing procedures.

GSM FREQUENCY ALLOCATION:

- GSM uses 900 MHz band.
- 890-960 MHz for the allocated for uplink and 935-960 MHz is allocated for downlink.
- Each way the bandwidth of GSM system is 25 MHz which provides 125 carriers uplink/downlink each having the bandwidth of 200 KHz.
- Absolute Radio Frequency Channel Number (ARFCN) denotes a forward and reverse channel pair which is separated in frequency by 4.5 MHz

Mobile-in base: F_t (n) =890.2+0.2(n-1) MHz
Base-to-mobile: F_t (n) = F_r (n) +45 MHz

- TDMA allows many users to share a common channel. The unit of time in TDMA is called a burst. Each user is assigned its own burst within a collection of bursts called a frame.
- GSM uses TDMA within a FDMA structure. As a result, different users can transmit using the same frequency, but they can't transmit at the same time. A 25MHz frequency band is divided using an FDMA scheme into 124 one-way carrier frequencies.
- Each base station is assigned one or more carriers to use in its cell. A 200 kHz frequency band separates the carrier frequencies from each other.
- Normally, a 25MHz band should be divisible into 125 carrier frequencies but in GSM the 1st carrier frequency is used as a guard band between GSM and other services that might be working on lower frequencies.

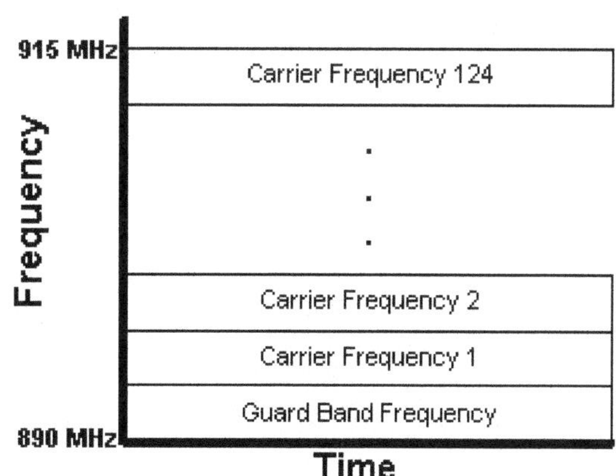

AUTHENTICATION AND SECURITY OF GSM:

Security in GSM:

- On air interface, GSM uses encryption and TMSI instead of IMSI.
- SIM is provided 4-8 digit PIN to validate the ownership of SIM
- 3 algorithms are specified :
    - A3 algorithm for authentication
    - A5 algorithm for encryption
    - A8 algorithm for key generation

1. A3 algorithm for authentication.

- Goal
    - Generation of SRES response to MSC's random challenge RAND.
    - Sim card uses this RAND received from the MSC and secret key is K_i stored with in SIM as input.
    - Both RAND and K_i secret are 128 bits long.
    - Using the A3 algorithm with RAND and K_i as input a 32-bit called SRES (signature response) is generated in the MS.
    - SRES sent back to the MSC as the response to them
    - Using the same set of algorithm, the AUC also generates a SRES.
    - The SRES from MS [SIM] and the SRES generated by the AUC are compared.
    - SRES values are calculated independently by the SIM.

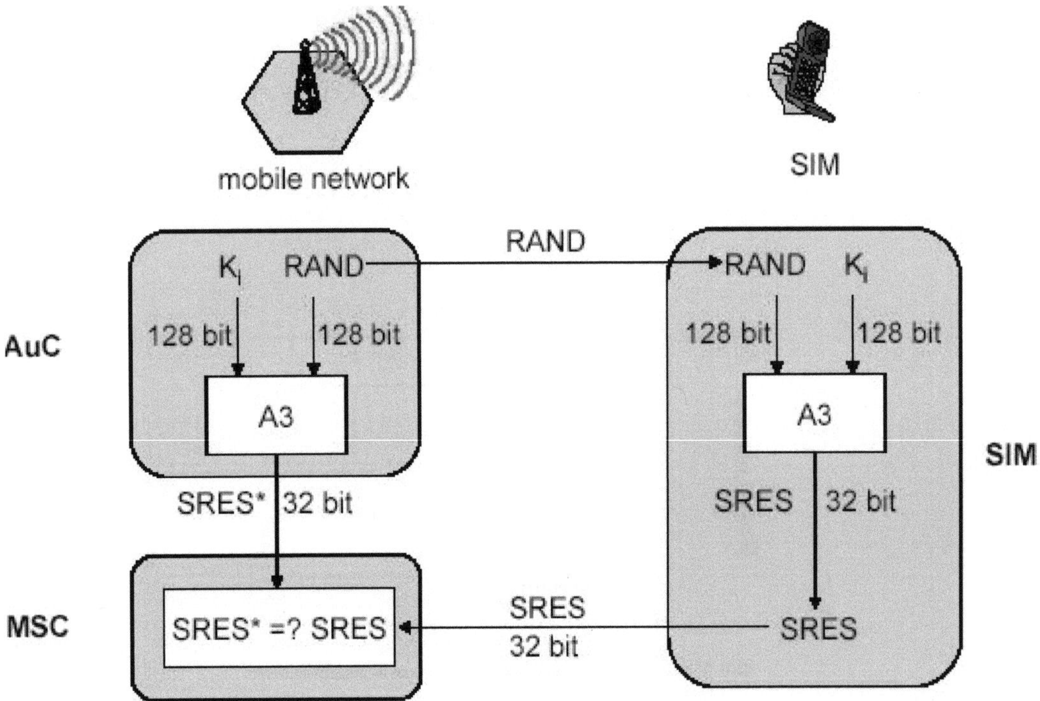

2. A8 algorithm for key generation

- Goal
  - Generation of session key K_s
    - A8 specification was never made public.
    - A8 generates the session key,K_c,from the random challenge ,RAND received from the secret key Ki.
    - The inputs for A8 ate same set of 128-bit $K_i$and RAND used in A3.
    - The A8 algorithm takes inputs and generates a 64-bit output.
    - The keys are generated at both the MS end and the network end.

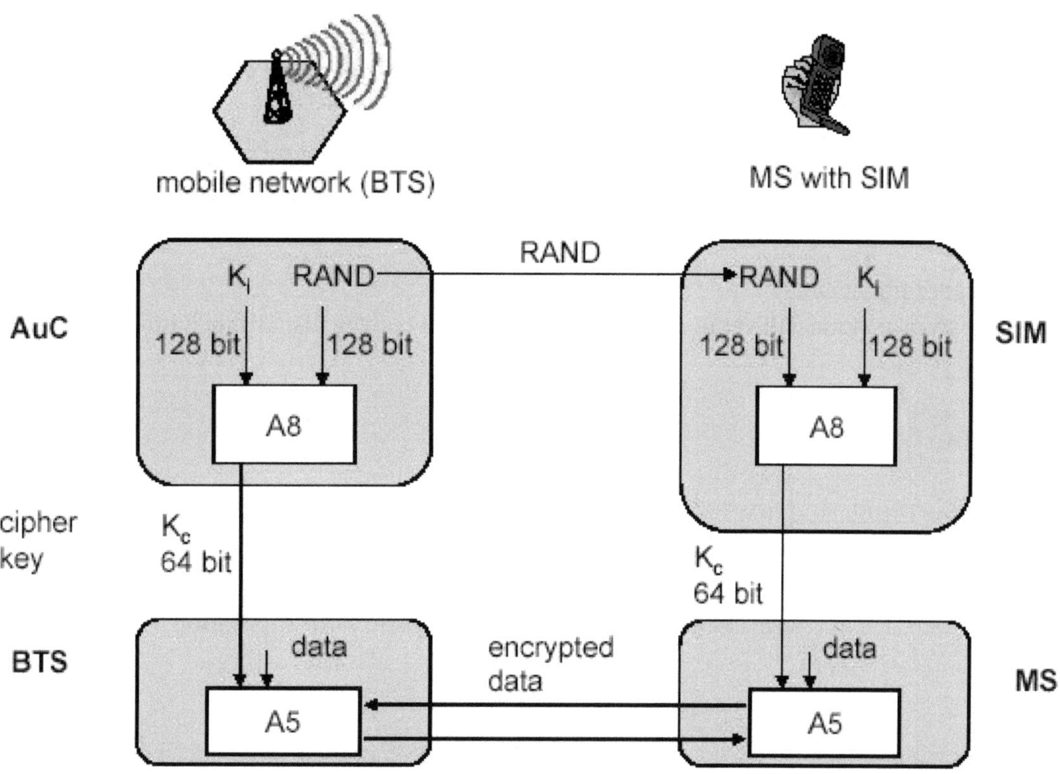

Enter Caption

SMS SERVICE:

- Short message service (SMS) is a globally accepted wireless service that enables the transmission of alphanumeric messages between mobile subscribers and external systems such as electronic mail, paging, and voice-mail systems.
- SMS appeared on the wireless scene in 1991 in Europe. The European standard for digital wireless, now known as the Global System for Mobile Communications (GSM), included short messaging services from the outset.
- In North America, SMS was made available initially on digital wireless networks built by early pioneers such as BellSouth Mobility, Prime Co, and Nextel, among others. These digital wireless networks are based on GSM, code division multiple access (CDMA), and time division multiple access (TDMA) standards.

Strengths of SMS:

1. An SMS is personal

Unlike an e-mail; an SMS is much more likely to be read by a person at any one time, since the majority of people have their mobile phones at arms reach 24 hours a day. Of course the same also applies to a phone call.

2. Messages are instantly recorded

Unlike a phone call; an SMS message is automatically stored where it can be re-read. This proves particularly useful in the case of fairly detailed information that might otherwise be forgotten. Here are a few everyday examples that would prove very handy via SMS rather than voice:

- odds on the 7 horses in the 4PM derby
- Directions to the 8PM party
- Your friends new mobile number

3. SMS messaging is relatively SPAM free

Unlike e-mail, SMS as it currently stands is relatively SPAM free. Although this may change over the next year or so, at present it is the ideal communication channel to cut through the clutter.

4. An SMS is Discreet

Unlike a phone call you do not have to run out of the restaurant where you are eating to field the call, yet you still know when an SMS has arrived. The discreet nature of text messaging ensures you stay in touch with minimal disturbance.

5. SMS leads to smaller phone bills

An SMS is far cheaper than a phone call yet in most instances you will convey just as much information as you would have if you had called.

SMS Architecture:

SMS are basically two types:

- Short Message Mobile Terminated (SMS-MT)/ Point-to-Point: the ability of a network to transmit a Short Message to a mobile phone. The message can be sent by phone or by a software application.
- Short Message Mobile Originated (SMS-MO)/ Point-to-Point: the ability of a network to transmit a Short Message sent by a mobile phone. The message can be sent to a phone or to a software application

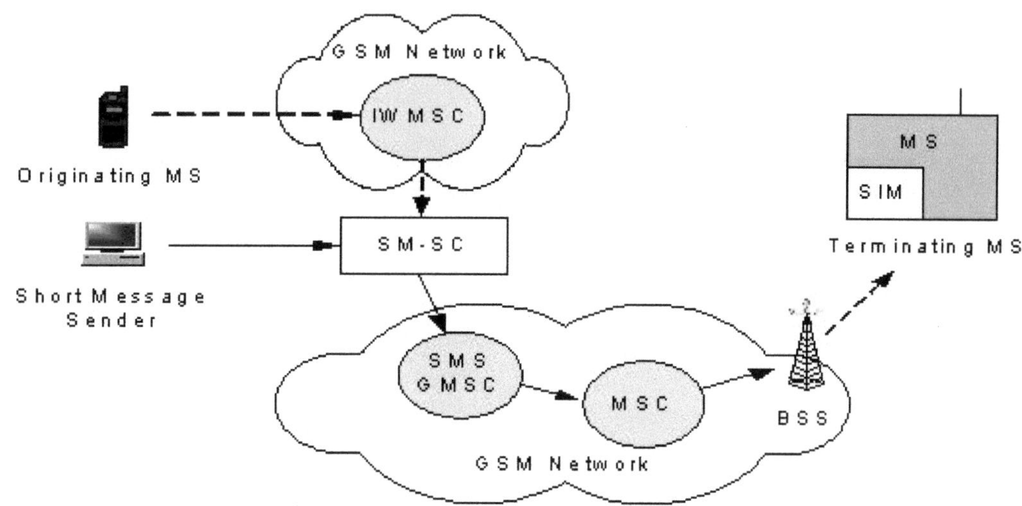

SMS GMSC : SMS Gateway MSC
IW MSC : Interworking MSC
SM-SC : Short Message Service Center
MSC : Mobile Switching Center
BSS : Base Station System
SIM : Subscriber Identity Module
MS : Mobile Station

SMPP:

- SMPP is an open, industry standard protocol designed to provide a flexible data communications interface for the transfer of short message data between External Short Message Entities (ESME), Routing Entities (RE) and Message Centers.
- The protocol is based on pairs of request/response PDUs (protocol data units, or packets) exchanged over OSI layer 4 (TCP session or X.25 SVC3) connections. PDUs are binary encoded for efficiency.
- Data exchange may be synchronous; where each peer must wait for a response for each PDU being sent, and asynchronous, where receiving and transmitting go in independent threads with the use of buffers and timers.

SMPP protocol overview:

- Short Message Peer to Peer (SMPP) protocol is an open message-transfer protocol that enables short message entities (SMEs) outside the mobile network to interface with an SMSC.

Nonmobile entities that submit messages to, or receive messages from an SMSC are known as External Short Message Entities (ESMEs).

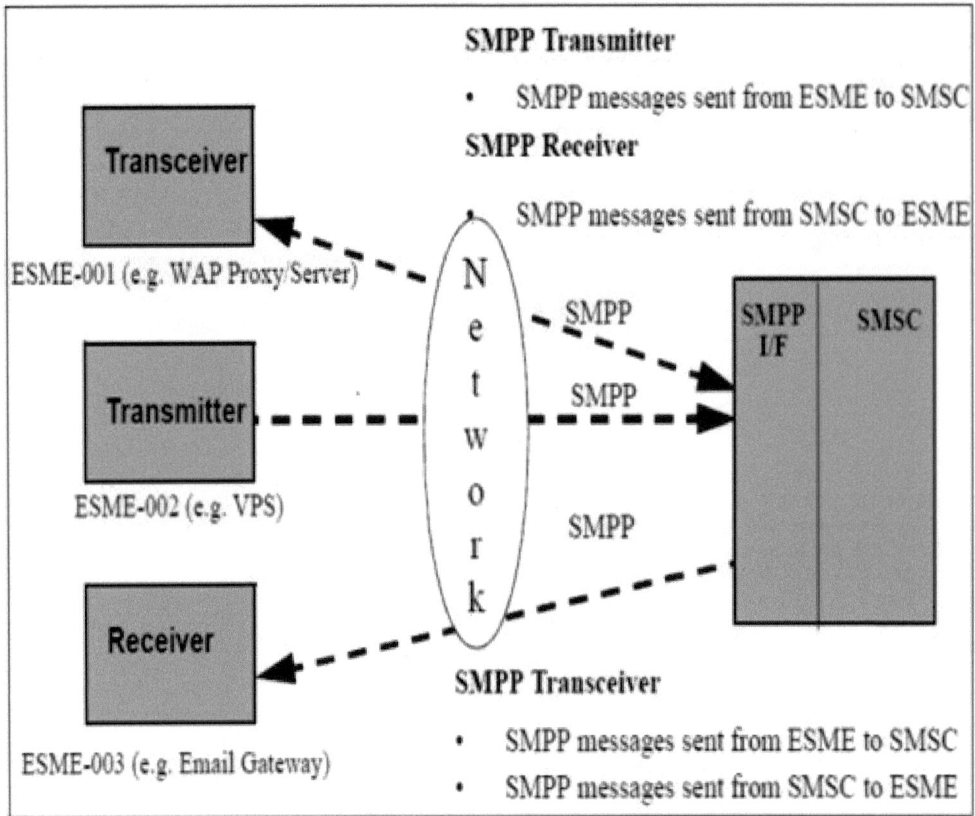

Figure 2-1: SMPP interface between SMSC and ESME

The SMPP protocol defines:

- a set of operations for the exchange of short messages between an ESME and an SMSC
- The data that an ESME application must exchange with an SMSC during SMPP operations.
- SMPP is based on the exchange of request and response protocol data units (PDUs) between the ESME and the SMSC over an underlying TCP/IP or X.25 network connection. The SMPP protocol defines:

1 .A set of operations and associated Protocol Data Units (PDUs) for the exchange of short messages between an ESME and an SMSC the data that an ESME application can exchange with an SMSC during SMPP operations.

- Note*Every SMPP operation must consist of a request PDU and associated response PDU.The receiving entity must return the associated SMPP response to an SMPP PDU request.
- The only exception to this rule is the ***alert notification*** PDU for which there is no response
- The exchange of messages between an ESME and SMSC via SMPP may be categorized under three distinct groups of transactions as follows:

1. Messages sent from the ESME (Transmitter) to the SMSC
2. Messages sent from the SMSC to the ESME (Receiver)
3. Messages sent from the ESME (Transceiver) to the SMSC and messages sent from the SMSC to the ESME (Transceiver)

The following Figure 2-1 illustrates the above categories, which are explained in more detail in subsequent sections.

CHAPTER IV

GPRS

GENERAL PACKET RADIO SERVICE (GPRS):

- **General packet radio service (GPRS)** is a packet oriented mobile data service on the 2G and 3G cellular communication systems global system for mobile communications (GSM).
- The service is available to users in over 200 countries worldwide.
- GPRS was originally standardized by European Telecommunications Standards Institute (ETSI) in response to the earlier CDPD and i-mode packet switched cellular technologies.
- It is now maintained by the 3rd Generation Partnership Project (3GPP).
- Part of GSM phase 2+
- General Packet Radio Service
    - General -> not restricted to GSM use (DECT ?, 3rd generation systems ?)
    - Packet Radio -> enables packet mode communication over air
    - Service, not System -> existing BSS (partially also NSS) infrastructure is used
- Requires many new network elements into NSS
- Provides connections to external packet data networks (Internet, X.25)
- Main benefits
    - Resources are reserved only when needed and charged accordingly
    - Connection setup times are reduced
    - Enables new service opportunities
- GPRS provides packet switched connections from MS to packet data networks (PDN)
- Different operator's GPRS networks are connected through Gp interface

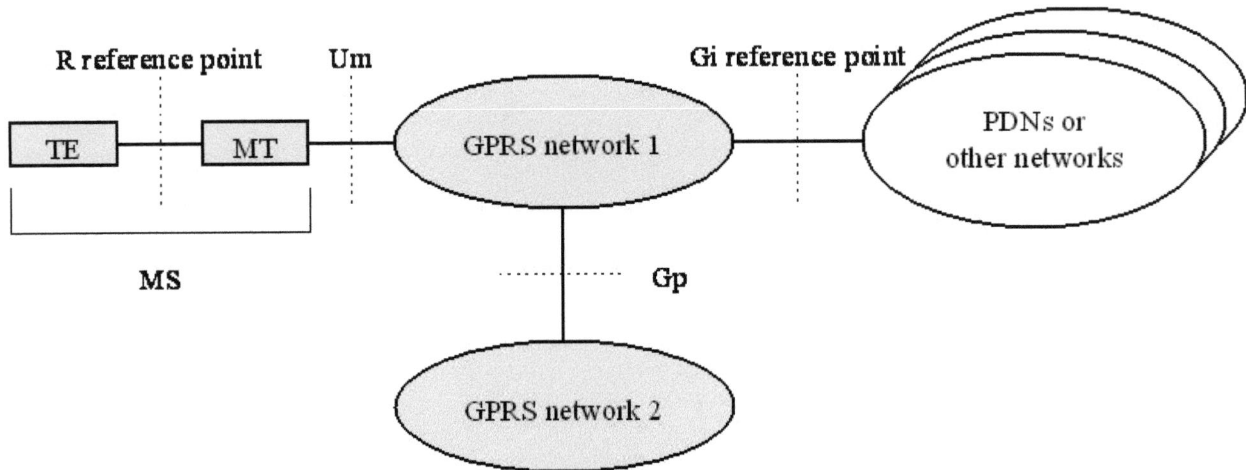

GPRS NETWORK ARCHITECTURE:

- It offers packet data services through GPRS, a new class of network nodes need to introduce in GSM network.
- The network nodes are called GPRS support nodes. (GSN).
- GPRS uses packet switched resource allocation
- resources allocated only when data is to be sent/received
- GPRS specific protocol based
- Point-to-point applications
- Toll road system, UIC train control system
- Point-to-multipoint applications
- Weather info, road traffic info, news, fleet management.

New network elements

1. GGSN
2. SGSN
3. Other elements
4. GPRS backbones.

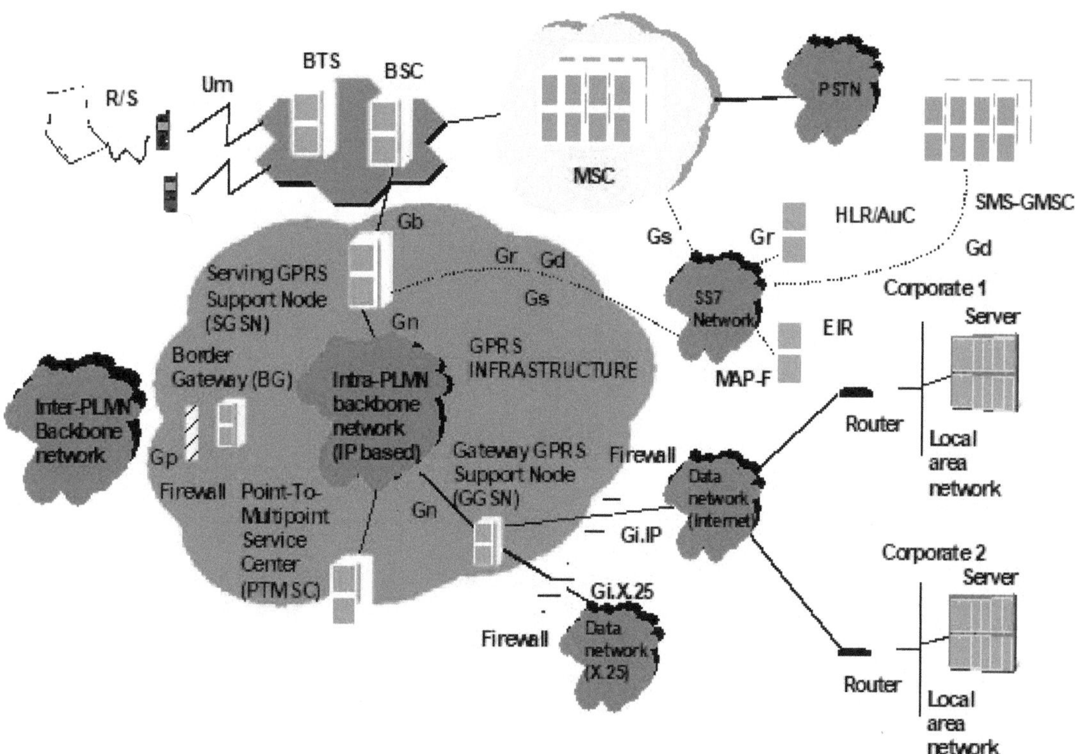

1. CGSN

- Typically located at one of the MSC sites
- One (or few) per operator
- Main functions
  - Interface to external data networks
  - Resembles to a data network router
  - Forwards end user data to right SGSN
  - Routes mobile originated packets to right destination

- Filters end user traffic
- Collects charging information for data network usage
- Data packets are not sent to MS unless the user has activated the PDP address

2. SGSN

- Functionally connected with BSC, physically can be at MSC or BSC site
- One for few BSCs or one (or few) per every BSC
- One SGSN can support BSCs of several MSC sites
- Main functions
  - Authenticates GPRS mobiles
  - Handles mobile's registration in GPRS network
  - Handles mobile's mobility management
  - Relays MO and MT data traffic
    - TCP/IP header compression, V.42bis data compression, error control MS- SGSN (ARQ)
  - Collect charging information of air interface usage

3. Other elements:
BG (Border Gateway)

- (Not defined within GPRS)
- Routes packets from SGSN/GGSN of one operator to a SGSN/GGSN of an other operator
- Provides protection against intruders from external networks

DNS (Domain Name Server)

- Translates addresses from ggsn1.oper1.fi -format to 123.45.67.89 format (i.e. as used in Internet)

4. GPRS backbones:

- Enables communication between GPRS Support Nodes
- Based on private IP network
  - IPv6 is the ultimate protocol
  - IPV4 can be used as an intermediate solution
- Intra-PLMN backbone
  - Connects GPRS Support Nodes of one operator
  - Operator decides the network architecture
    - LAN, point-to-point links, ATM, ISDN, ...
- Inter-PLMN backbone

- Connects GPRS operators via BGs
- Provides international GPRS roaming
- Operators decide the backbone in the roaming agreement

GPRS NETWORK OPERATION:

1. GPRS Attachment and detachment procedure:

GPRS Attach

- In order to access GPRS services, an MS performs an IMSI attach for GPRS services to signal its presence to the network.
- During the attach procedure, the MS provides its identity, either a temporary identifier or *packet temporary mobile station identity* (P-TMSI) previously allocated by the SGSN, or an IMSI identifier when P-TMSI is not valid.
- When the MS is GPRS-attached, an MM context is established between the MS and the SGSN. This means that information related to this MS (i.e., IMSI, P-TMSI, cell identity, and RA) is stored in the SGSN.
- A GPRS-attached mobile is localized by the network at least at RA level and may be paged at any moment in GMM STANDBY state.

GPRS Detach

- A GPRS MS can no longer access GPRS service when it is GPRS-detached. The detach may be explicit or implicit.
- It is explicit when signaling is exchanged between the MS and the network.
- The detach is implicit when the network detaches the MS without any notification, and it may occur when the network does not detect any activity related to the MS for a certain amount of time.

2. Routing:

- The main functions of the GGSN involve interaction with the external data network.
- The GGSN updates the location directory using routing information supplied by the SGSNs about the location of an MS.
- It routes the external data network protocol packet encapsulated over the GPRS backbone to the SGSN currently serving the MS.
- It also decapsulates and forwards external data network packets to the appropriate data network and collect charging data that is forwarded to a charging gateway (CG).

There are three important routing schemes:

- **Mobile-originated message:** This path begins at the GPRS mobile and ends at the host
- **Network-initiated message when the MS is in its home network:** This path begins at the host and ends at the GPRS mobile
- **Network-initiated message when the MS roams to another GPRS network:** This path begins at the host of visited network and ends at the GPRS mobile

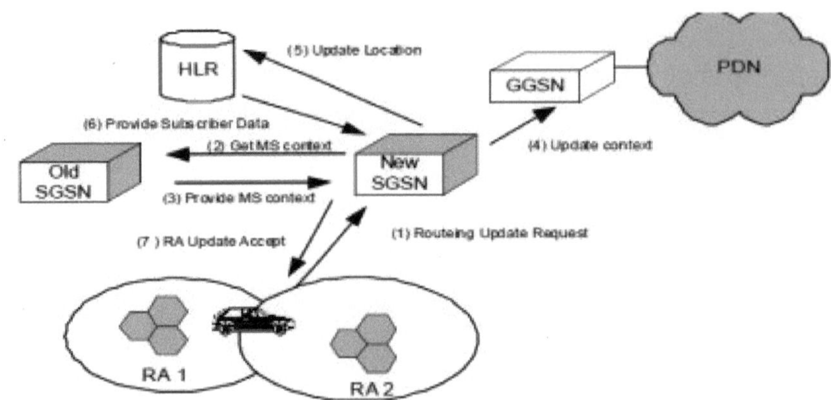

FIGURE 9. Inter-SGSN Routeing Update Procedure (simplified)

3. Mobility Management:

- The operation of the GPRS is partly independent of the GSM network. However, some procedures share the network elements with current GSM functions to increase efficiency and to make optimum use of free GSM resources (such as unallocated time slots).
- An MS can be any of the following three states in the GPRS system. The three-state model is unique to packet radio. GSM uses a two-state model either idle or active.
- Instead of Location Area, GPRS uses Routing Areas to group cells. RA is a subset of LA.

- IDLE:
    - MS is not known by the network (SGSN)
- STANDBY:
    - MS's location is known in accuracy of Routing Area
    - MS can utilize DRX (to save battery)
    - MS must inform its location after every Routing Area change (no need to inform if MS changes from one cell to another within same Routing Area)
    - Before the network can perform MT data transfer MS must be paged within the Routing Area
    - MS may initiate MO data transfer at any time
- READY:
    - MS's location is known in accuracy of cell
    - MS must inform its location after every cell change
    - MS can initiate MO data transfer at any time
    - SGSN does not need to page the MS before MT data transfer
    - MS listens continuously GPRS PCCCH channel
        - DRX in READY state is optional

<u>**DATA SERVICES IN GPRS:**</u>

There are two modes in GPRS network:

- Application mode.
- Tunneling mode.

Application mode.

- The user will be using the GPRS mobile phone to access the applications running on the phone itself. The phone act as an end user device.

Tunneling mode.

- The mobile phone is connected to the device and used as a modem to access the wireless network.

1. GPRS handsets:

- The handset is probably the most well-known piece of equipment, because this is the part we use to make phone calls and to access data services.
- When we talk about advanced services, the handset is commonly called an MS, which consists of terminal equipment (TE) and a mobile terminal (MT).
- TE is the device that hosts the applications and the user interaction, while the MT is the part that connects to the network.

In the following example Palm Pilot is TE and Mobile phone is MT.

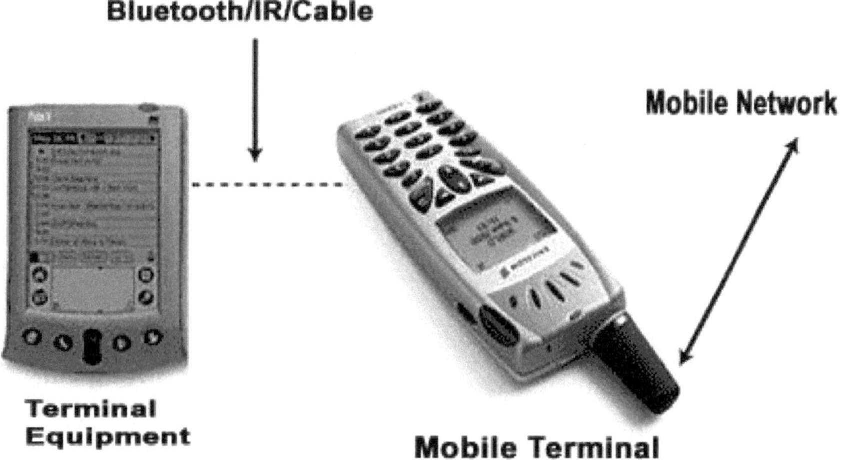

Enter Caption

In order to take advantage of the new GPRS services, we need new GPRS enabled handsets. There are three different classes of GPRS terminal equipments.

Class A:

- Class A terminals can handle packet data and voice at the same time. In other words, we need two transceivers because the handset has to send and/or receive data and voice at the same time.
- This situation makes class A terminals significantly more expensive to manufacture than class B and C terminals.

Class B:

- Class B terminals can handle both packet data and voice, but not at the same time. In other words, you can use the same transceiver for both, keeping the cost of the terminals down.
- In practice, the GPRS session (like WAP browsing, file transfer, and so on) is suspended when a GSM voice call is started.. That way, a user who is transferring money between his or her accounts by using a WAP service does not have to stop that transaction just because someone calls.

Class C:

- Class C terminals can only handle either voice or data.
- Examples of class C terminals are GPRS PCM/CIA cards, embedded modules in vending machines, and so on.

2. Bearears in GPRS:

It offers end to end packet switched data transfer.

There are two kinds of data transport services:

1. Point-to Point service (PTM).
2. Point-to-multipoint service(PTM)

GPRS also support other types of services:

1. **SMS-originally designed as a GSM network.**
2. **WAP-It provide services over HTTP protocol.**
3. **MMS-supports multimedia messages.**

GPRS APPLICATIONS:

GPRS enables a variety of new and unique services to the mobile wireless subscriber. These mobile services have unique characteristics that provide enhanced value to customers. These characteristics include the following:

- **Mobility:** The ability to maintain constant voice and data communications while on the move
- **Immediacy** Allows subscribers to obtain connectivity when needed, regardless of location and without a lengthy login session.
- **Localization** Allows subscribers to obtain information relevant to their current location.

The combination of these characteristics provides a wide spectrum of possible applications that can be offered to mobile subscribers. In general, applications can be separated into two high-level categories: corporate and consumer. These include:

- **Communications:** E-mail, fax, unified messaging and intranet/Internet access etc.

- **Value-added services:** Information services and games etc.
- **E-commerce:** Retail, ticket purchasing, banking and financial trading etc.
- **Location-based applications:** Navigation, traffic conditions, airline/rail schedules and location finder etc.
- **Vertical applications:** Freight delivery, fleet management and sales-force automation.
- **Advertising:** Advertising may be location sensitive. For example, a user entering a mall can receive advertisements specific to the stores in that mall.

It is also possible to send SMS messages over GPRS. In addition, it is planned to implement supplementary services, such as call forwarding unconditional (CFU), call forwarding on mobile subscriber not reachable (CFNRc), and closed user group (CUG).

<u>LIMITATIONS OF GPRS:</u>

However, it is important to note that there are some limitations with GPRS, which can be summarized as:

1. Limited Cell Capacity for All Users:

- GPRS does impact a network's existing cell capacity
- There are only limited radio resources it can be deployed for different uses - use for one purpose precludes simultaneous use for another
- For example, voice and GPRS calls both use the same network resources. The extent of the impact depends upon the number of timeslots, if any, that are reserved for exclusive use of GPRS.

2. Speeds Much Lower in Reality:

- Achieving the theoretical maximum GPRS data transmission speed of 172.2 kbps would require a single user taking over all eight timeslots without any error protection.
- Clearly, it is unlikely that a network operator will allow all timeslots to be used by a single GPRS user. Additionally, the initial GPRS terminals are expected be severely limited - supporting only one, two or three timeslots.

3. Support of GPRS Mobile Terminate by Terminals is not ensured:

- At the time of writing, there has been no confirmation from any handset vendors that mobile terminated GPRS calls (i.e. receipt of GPRS calls on the mobile phone) will be supported by the initial GPRS terminals.
- Availability or not of GPRS MT is a central question with critical impact on the GPRS business case such as application migration from other non voice bearers.

<u>BILLING AND CHARGING IN GPRS:</u>

BILLING:

- GPRS is a different kind of service from those typically available on today's mobile networks.
- GPRS is essentially a packet switching overlay on a circuit switching network. The GPRS specifications stipulate the minimum charging information that must be collected in the Stage 1 service description.
- These include destination and source addresses, usage of radio interface, usage of external Packet Data Networks, usage of the packet data protocol addresses, usage of general GPRS resources and location of the Mobile Station.
- Since GPRS networks break the information to be communicated down into packets, at a minimum, a GPRS network needs to be able to count packets to charging customers for the volume of packets they send and receive.
- Today's billing systems have difficulties handling charging for today's non voice services. It is unlikely that circuit switched billing systems will be able to process a large number of new variables created by GPRS.

TARRIFING:

- Decisions on charging for GPRS by packet or simply a flat monthly fee are contentious but need to be made.
- Charging different packets at different rates can make things complicated for the user, whilst flat rates favor heavy users more than occasional ones.
- We believe that the optimal GPRS pricing model will be based on two variables - time and packet.
- Network operators should levy a nominal per packet charge during peak times plus a flat rate, no per packet charge during non peak times.
- Time and packet related charging will encourage applications such as remote monitoring, meter reading and chat to use GPRS overnight when spare network capacity is available.
- Simultaneously, a nominal per packet charge during the day will help to allocate scarce radio resources and charge radio heavy applications such as file and image transfer more than applications with lower data intensity.
- It has the advantage that it will automatically adjust customer charging according to their application usage.

WAP:

Introduction: Wireless Application Protocol (**WAP**) is a technical standard for accessing information over a mobile wireless network. A WAP browser is a web browser for mobile devices such as mobile phones that uses the protocol.

- Empowers mobile users with wireless devices to easily access and interact with information and services.
- A "standard" created by wireless and Internet companies to enable Internet access from a cellular phone

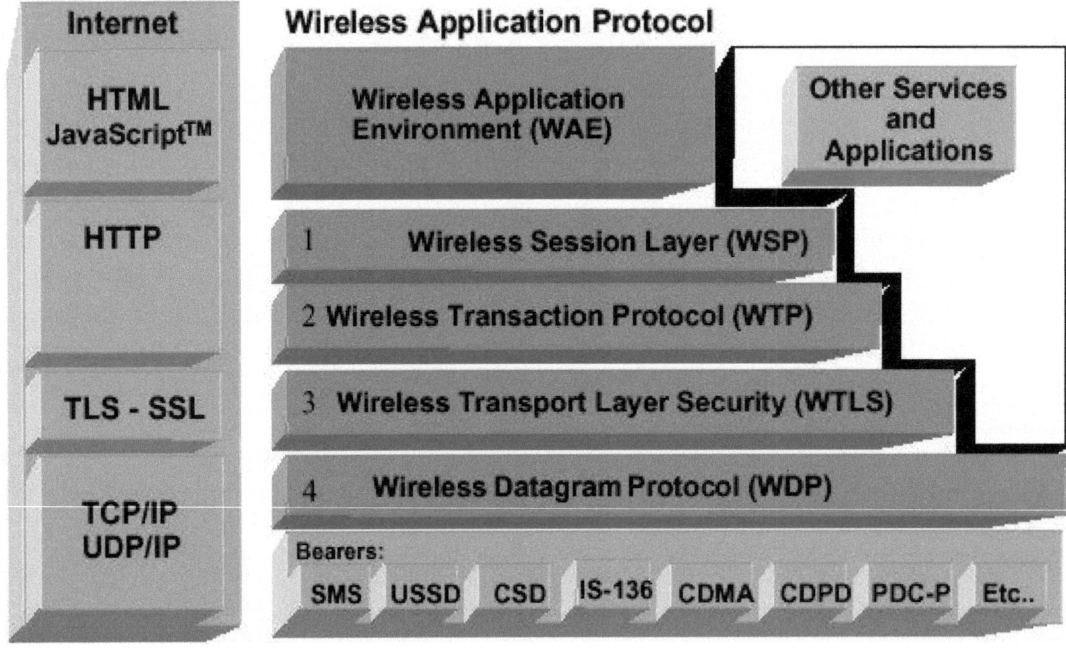

- WAE (Wireless Application Environment):
  - Architecture: application model, browser, gateway, server
  - WML: XML-Syntax, based on card stacks, variables.
  - WTA: telephone services, such as call control phone book etc.

- WSP (Wireless Session Protocol):
    - Provides HTTP 1.1 functionality
    - Supports session management, security, etc.
- WTP (Wireless Transaction Protocol):
    - Provides reliable message transfer mechanisms
    - Based on ideas from TCP/RPC
- WTLS (Wireless Transport Layer Security):
    - Provides data integrity, privacy, authentication functions
    - Based on ideas from TLS/SSL
- WDP (Wireless Datagram Protocol):
    - Provides transport layer functions
    - Based on ideas from UDP

Wireless Application Environment (WAE):

- Goals
    - device and network independent application environment
    - for low-bandwidth, wireless devices
    - considerations of slow links, limited memory, low computing power, small display, simple user interface (compared to desktops)
    - integrated Internet/WWW programming model
    - high interoperability

WAE model includes:

- User Agents
    - WML/WTA/Others
    - Content formats: vCard, vCalendar, Wireless Bitmap, WML.
- WML
    - XML-Syntax, based on card stacks, variables, ...
- WML Script
    - procedural, loops, conditions, ... (similar to JavaScript)
- WTA

- telephone services, such as call control, text messages, phone book, ... (accessible from WML/WML Script)

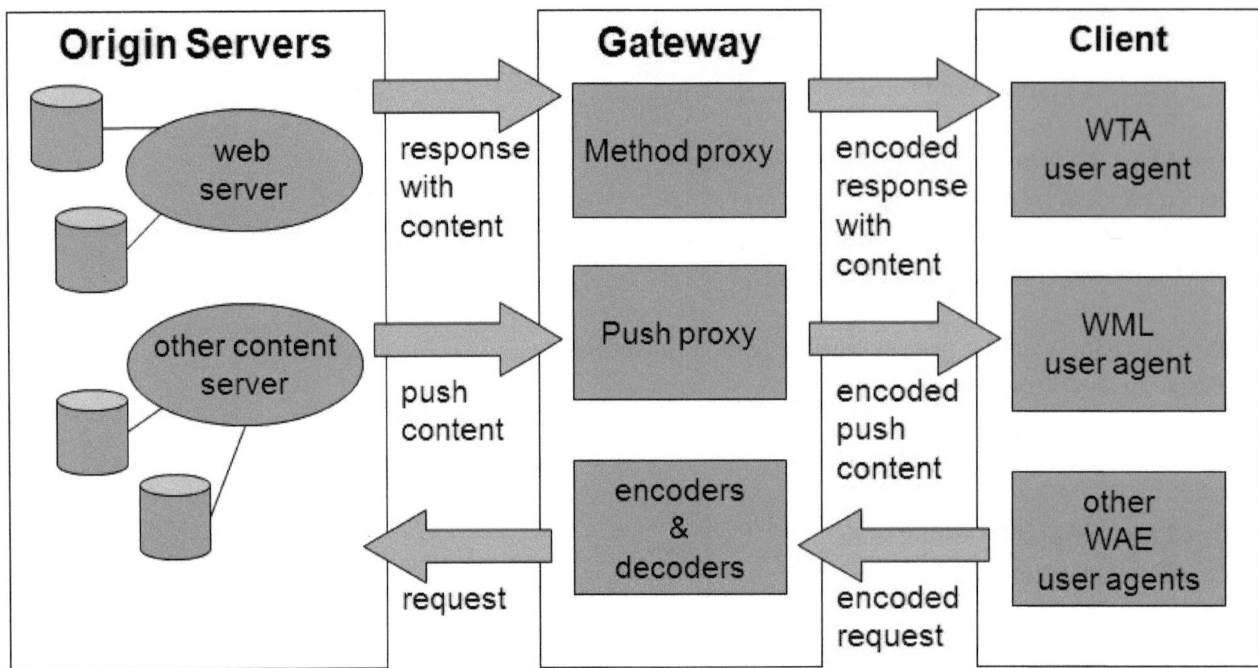

MMS:

- MMS is short for Multimedia Messaging Service .Its biggest feature is supported for multimedia functions, to pass full-featured content and information that include text, images, voice, data and other multimedia formats.
- MMS is technically not a real message, but in the GPRS network with the support of the WAP wireless application protocol as a carrier to send pictures, sound and text information.
- MMS can achieve instant end to end mobile phones, mobile terminals to the Internet or the Internet to the mobile terminal of the multimedia messaging.

MMS ARCHITECTURE:

- A key feature of MMS is the ability to support messaging activities with other available messaging systems. This is shown in Figure 2 below which shows an abstract view of an MMS network diagram.
- It is expected that specific MMS networks may have one or more such connections as well as include specific messaging services not directly represented (e.g. fax or voice mail systems).

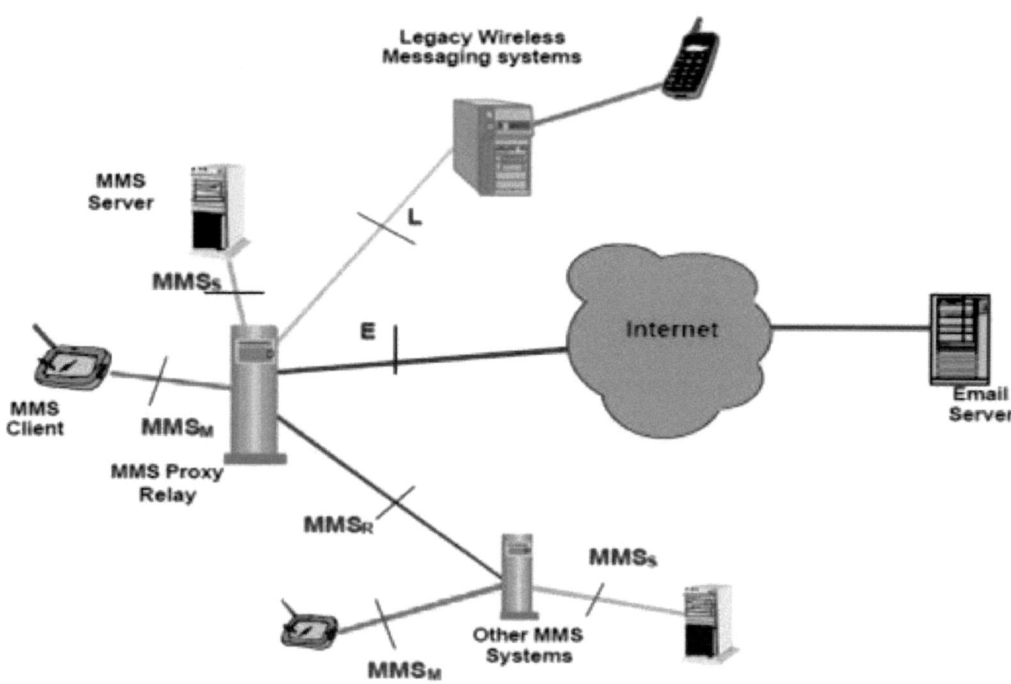

Figure 2 MMS Network Representation

The system elements shown in Figure 2 can be summarized as follows:

MMS Client – This is the system element that interacts with the user. It is expected to be implemented as an application on the user's wireless device.

MMS Proxy-Relay – This is the system element that the MMS Client interacts with. It provides access to the components that provide message storage services, and it is responsible for messaging activities with other available messaging systems. Some implementations may combine this component with the MMS Server.

MMS Server – This system element provides storage services for MM messages. Some implementations may combine this component with the MMS Proxy -Relay.

Email Server – This system element provides traditional Internet email services. It supports the SMTP protocol to send messages as well as POP and/or IMAP protocols to retrieve messages.

Legacy Wireless Messaging Systems – This system element represents various systems that currently existing support of wireless messaging systems. This would include paging and SMS systems that provide messaging to a large number of subscribers.

SMIL:

This document specifies the third version of the Synchronized Multimedia Integration Language (SMIL, pronounced "smile"). SMIL 3.0 has the following design goals:

- Define an XML-based language that allows authors to write interactive multimedia presentations. Using SMIL, an author may describe the temporal behavior of a multimedia presentation, associate hyperlinks with media objects and describe the layout of the presentation on a screen.
- Allow reusing of SMIL syntax and semantics in other XML-based languages, in particular those who need to represent timing and synchronization. For example, SMIL components are used for integrating timing into XHTML [XHTML10] and into SVG [SVG].

- Extend the functionalities contained in the SMIL 2.1 [SMIL21] into new or revised SMIL 3.0 modules.
- Define new SMIL 3.0 Profiles incorporating features useful within the industry.

EXAMPLE:

```
<smil>
<head>
<meta name="title" content="SMIL Wrapper"/>
<layout>
<root-layout background-color="black"
height=" 315"
width=" 325"/>
<region id="video region"
background-color="black"
top=" 5"
left=" 5"
height=" 240"
width=" 320"/>
<region id="textregion"
background-color="black"
top=" 255"
left=" 5"
height=" 60"
width=" 320"/>
</layout>
</head>
<body>
<par>
<!-- VIDEO -->
<video src="v-hi.mpg" region="videoregion"/>

<!-- CAPTIONS -->
<switch>
<textstream src="v-hi.rt"
region="textregion"
system-language="en"
system-captions="on"
title="english captions"
alt="english captions"/>
</switch>
</par>
</body>
</smil>
```

CHAPTER V

CDMA AND 3G

SPREAD-SPECTRUM TECHNOLOGY:

- **Spread-spectrum** techniques are methods by which a signal (e.g. an electrical, electromagnetic, or acoustic signal) generated in a particular bandwidth is deliberately spread in the frequency domain, resulting in a signal with a wider bandwidth.
- These techniques are used for a variety of reasons, including the establishment of secure communications, increasing resistance to natural interference and jamming, to prevent detection, and to limit power flux density
- **Spread spectrum** is a communication technique that spreads a narrowband communication signal over a wide range of frequencies for transmission then de-spreads it into the original data bandwidth at the receive.
- **Spread spectrum** is characterized by:

- wide bandwidth and
- low power

- **Jamming** and **interference** have less effect on Spread spectrum because it is:

1. Resembles noise
2. Hard to detect à Hard to intercept

1. Narrow Band

- Uses only enough frequency spectrum to carry the signal
- High peak power

1. Easily jammed

Narrowband *vs* Spread Spectrum

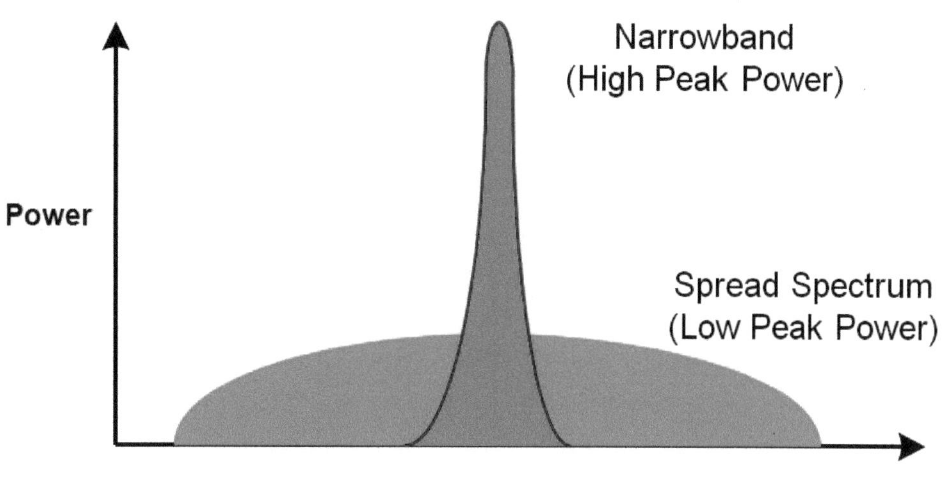

1. **Spread Spectrum**

- The bandwidth is much wider than required to send to the signal.
- Low peak power
- Hard to detect
- Hard to intercept
- Difficult to jam.

Direct Sequence Spread Spectrum (DSSS):

1. DSSS works by combining information ***bits*** (data signal) with higher data rate bit sequence (***pseudorandom number (PN)***).
2. The PN is also called a ***Chipping Code*** (eg., the Barker chipping code)
3. The bits resulting from combining the information bits with the chipping code are called ***chips*** - the result- which is then transmitted.

   - The higher ***processing gain*** (more chips) increases the signal's resistance to interference by spreading it across a greater number of frequencies.
   - IEEE has set their **minimum processing gain to 11.** The number of chips in the chipping code equates to the signal **spreading ratio.**
   - Doubling the chipping speed doubles the signal spread and the required bandwidth.

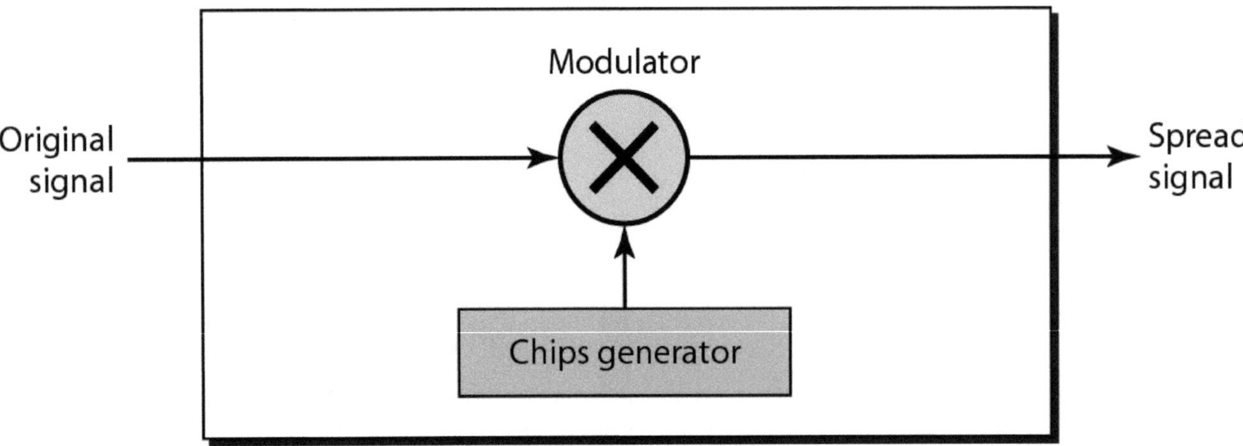

Walsh function:

- In mathematical analysis, the set of **Walsh functions** form an orthogonal basis of the square-integral functions on the unit interval. The functions take the values -1 and +1 only, on sub-intervals defined by dyadic fractions. They are useful in electronics, and other engineering applications.
- The orthogonal Walsh functions are used to perform the Hadamard transform, which is very similar to the way the orthogonal sinusoids are used to perform the Fourier transform.

- The Walsh functions are related to the Haar functions; both form a complete orthogonal system. The Haar function system may on the one hand be preferable because of its wavelet properties (e.g. localization), on the other hand the Walsh functions are bounded (in fact of modulus 1 everywhere).
- The order of the function is 2^s, where *s* is an integer, meaning that there are 2^s (time-) intervals in which the value is -1 or 1.
- A list of the 2^s Walsh functions make a Hadamard matrix.
- One way to define Walsh functions is using the binary digit representations of reals and integers. For an integer *k* consider the binary digit representation

  - $k = k_0 + k_1 2 + \ldots + k_m 2^m$,

- for some integer *m*, and with k_i equal to 0 or 1. Then if *k* is the Gray code transform of *j-1*, the *j*-th **Walsh function** at a point *x*, with $0 \leq x < 1$, is

  - $wal_j(x) = (-1)^{(k_0 x_0 + \ldots k_m x_m)}$,

- if

  - $x = x_0/2 + x_1/2^2 + x_2/2^3 + \ldots$,

- Where again x_i is 0 or 1 (only finitely often 1, if *x* is a dyadic number).
- Walsh functions can be interpreted as the characters of

  - $(\mathbf{Z}_2)^N$,

- The group of sequences over $\mathbf{Z}_2$; using this viewpoint, several generalizations have been defined.
- Applications (in mathematics) can be found wherever digit representations are used, e.g. in the analysis of digital quasi-Monte Carlo methods.
- Walsh functions are used in Radio Astronomy to reduce the effects of electrical crosstalk between antenna signals

IS-95:

- **Interim Standard 95 (IS-95)** is the first CDMA-based digital cellular standard by Qualcomm.
- The brand name for IS-95 is **cdmaOne**. IS-95 is also known as TIA-EIA-95.
- It is a 2G Mobile Telecommunications Standard that uses CDMA, a multiple access scheme for digital radio, to send voice, data and signaling data (such as a dialed telephone number) between mobile telephones and cell sites.
- CDMA or "code division multiple access" is a digital radio system that transmits streams of bits (PN codes).
- CDMA permits several radios to share the same frequencies.
- Unlike TDMA "time division multiple access", a competing system used in 2G GSM, all radios can be active all the time, because network capacity does not directly limit the number of active radios.

- CDMA is an access method.
- IS-95 was the first 'operating system' to use CDMA

  - Invented by Qualcomm
  - Began production in 1995.
  - At this point, this is still called 2G wireless.

    - Known as a narrowband system.

- Being supplanted by CDMA2000 (WCDMA) and UMTS, fully 3G systems.
    - They both use CDMA.
    - Known as wideband systems.
- Operates in the same bandwidth as GSM:
    - 1850 to 1910 MHz Mobile to Base
    - 1930 – 1990 MHz Base to Mobile
- Channels are 1.25 MHz
    - 3.75 MHz in CDMA 2000, 5 MHZ in UMTS
    - Results in approximately only 48 forward/reverse channel pairs in IS-95.
- Adjacent cell phone towers use the exact same channels as all other towers.
    - This is a major difference.

Allows for much better frequency reuse and makes setting up a cellular network much easier

- When a phone is turned on, it scans one of the forward channels to find a base station identifier.
    - Camps on the strongest signal.
- The phone sends out an encrypted pass key and gains access to the network.
- It can then sends and receive calls.
    - It is assigned a 1.25 MHz wide frequency to operate on.
- It listens for pages on the forward channel to let it know it has a call incoming.
- This is all very similar to how GSM operates so far.

IS-95 Architecture:
The main elements of reference model:

- Mobile station(MS):

- This is a mobile phone with user.
- The MS terminate the radio path on the user side and enable the user to gain access the service from network.

- Base station(BS):

- It terminates the radio path and connects to the mobile switching center.
- BS is a system between MS and MSC.

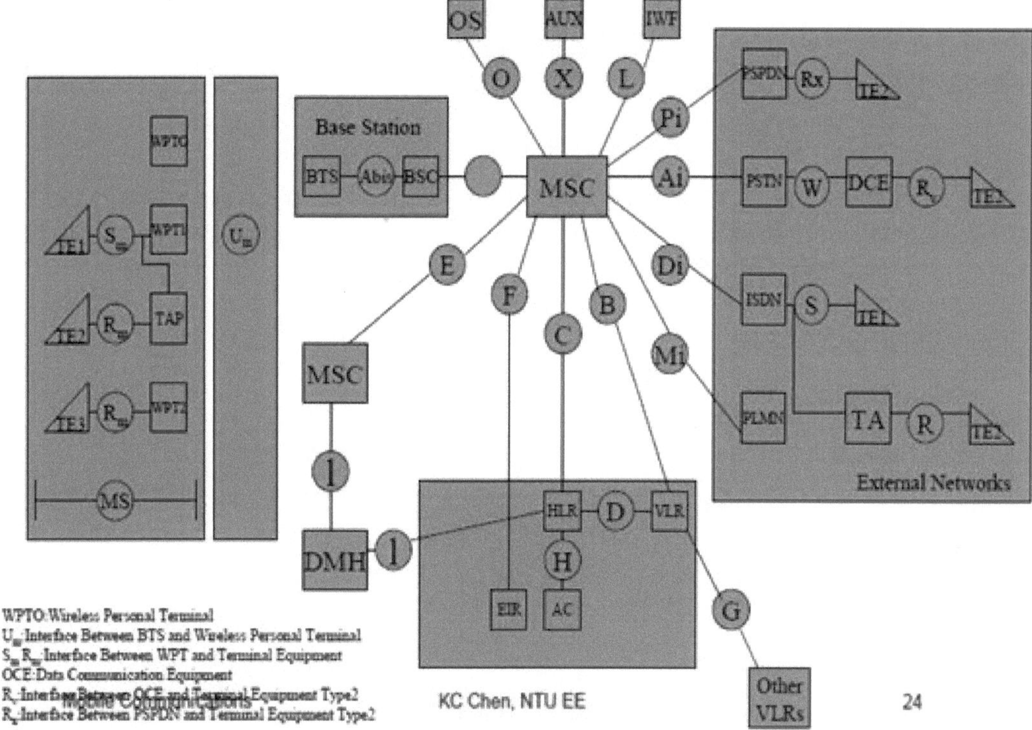

BS is segmented into

Base Transceiver Station (BTS): consists of one or more transceivers placed at a single location.

Base Station Controller (BSC): It is a control and management system for one or more BTSs.

- It exchange messages may pass through BSC transparency.
- Mobile switching Center(MSC):
- It is an automatic system that interfaces the user traffic from the wireless network with the wire line network or other wireless networks.
- Home location Register(HLR):

  It is responsible for overall management of wireless network.
- Internetworking Function (IWF): It is a functional unit that manages mobile subscribers by maintaining all subscriber related information.
- One HLR can serve multiple MSCs or may be distributed over multiple locations.
- Data Message Handler(DMH):

- It is responsible for collating the billing data.

- Visited Location Register(VLR):

- It is functional unit that dynamically stores subscriber information obtained from the subscribers HLR data.
- It is considered as cache.

- Authentication Center(AC):

- It manages the authentication associated with individual subscriber.
- The AC may be located with HLR or MSC.

- Equipment Identity Register(EIR):

- It provides the information about the mobile device for record purpose.
- EIR may be located with MSC or located independent of it.

- Operating System(OS)

- It enables the MSC to communicate with other networks.

IS-95 Channel Structure:

Structure of IS-95 channels in the forward link:

This is a total of 64 IS-95 code channels that can be accommodated on each RF channel. The IS-95 channels in the forward link are arranged in the following fashion:

- Pilot channel
- Paging channels (up to seven)
- Sync channel
- Traffic channels

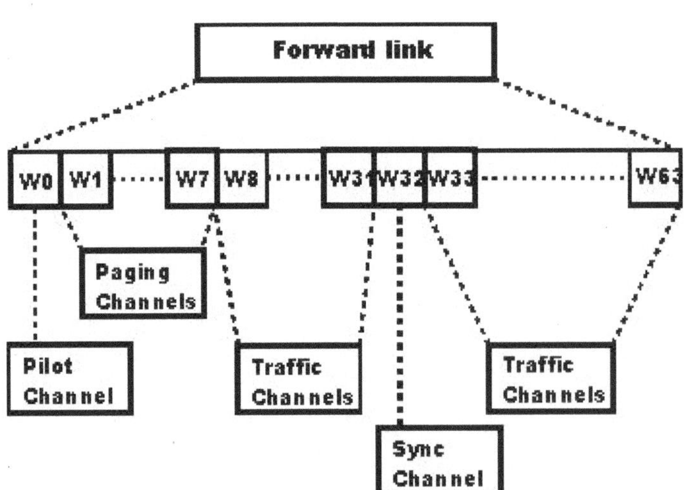

IS-95 channels in the forward link with associated Walsh codes

- To generate the final signal, the data from the individual channels is multiplied with the Walsh codes to provide the individual IS-95 forward link channels.
- The output from this process is then further multiplied with the short PN codes.
- This provides a means of identifying the sector / cell from which the signal is coming for the handset / mobile.

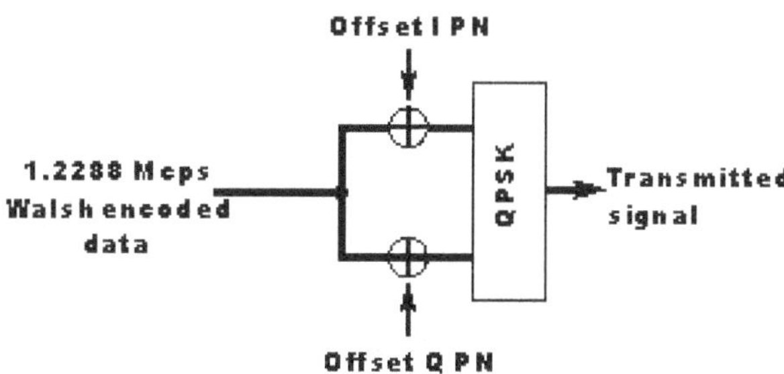

IS-95 channels forward link spreading

IS-95 channels in the forward link

The IS-95 forward link channels and their functions and make-up are summarized below:

- *Pilot channel (PC):* The pilot channel is transmitted as a reference by the base station to provide timing and phase reference for the mobiles, and carries no real data.. This means that the pilot channel is effectively the PN sequence with its associated offset.
- *Paging channels (PCH):*

- This IS-95 channel is used to carry information to enable mobiles to be paged.
- Data carried by this IS-95 channel includes system parameters, voice pages, SMS and other broadcast messages.
- It occupies Walsh codes 1 - 7 dependent upon the system requirements.
- *Synchronisation channel (SC):*
- This IS-95 channel is used to provide the timing reference to access the cell.
- This IS-95 channel always uses Walsh code 32. Each base station has a fixed timing offset to reduce the interference between adjacent base-stations.

- *Forward Traffic Channel (FTC):*

- The Forward Traffic Channel is used to carry voice, user data, and also signalling information.
- When carrying voice, the coded voice data does not require a constant bit rate and IS-95 allows the rate of the frames to change dynamically (every 20 ms).
- When the rate is reduced it reduces the level of interference to other users. The original vectored specification used a set of rates based on divisions of 9.6 kbps.

- *Access channel (AC):*

This IS-95 channel is used by the mobile to communicate with the base station when no traffic channel has been set up.

- There can be up to 32 Access Channels on the IS-95 reverse link for each Paging Channel on forward link.

- *Reverse traffic channel (RTC):* Like the Forward Traffic Channel, this reverse link IS-95 channel is used to carry variable rate voice data, user data and signaling.

IS-95 calls processing:

- IS-95 CDMA calls processing states that a mobile station goes through in getting to traffic channel.
- These include the system initialization state, the system idle state, the system access state, and the traffic channel state.

1. System initialization state à the mobile acquires the pilot channel by searching all the PN offsets possibilities and selecting the strongest pilot (W_0) signal.
2. Idle state à it monitors the paging channel.
3. Access state à if a call is placed or received mobile enters **access state** necessary parameters are exchanged.
4. Traffic state à if access attempt is successful state voice or data is transacted.

CDMA Registration

- The registration process is used by the mobile to notify the base station of its location, status, identification, slot cycle, and other characteristics. The base station can efficiently page the mobile station when establishing a mobile-terminated call.

Handoff and Roaming:

- The handoff is initiated and executed without the user attempting to have simultaneous traffic channel communications with the two base stations.
- With soft handoff, a conditional decision is made on whether to hand off. Depending on the changes in pilot signal strength from the two or more base stations involved, a hard decision will eventually be made to communicate with only one.
- This normally happens after it is evident that the signal from one base station is considerably stronger than those from the others.
- Types of hand-off
- Intersector or softer handoff.

The mobile communicates with two sectors of the same cell (see Fig).

- A RAKE receiver at the base station combines the best versions of the voice frame from the diversity antennas of the two sectors into a single traffic frame.

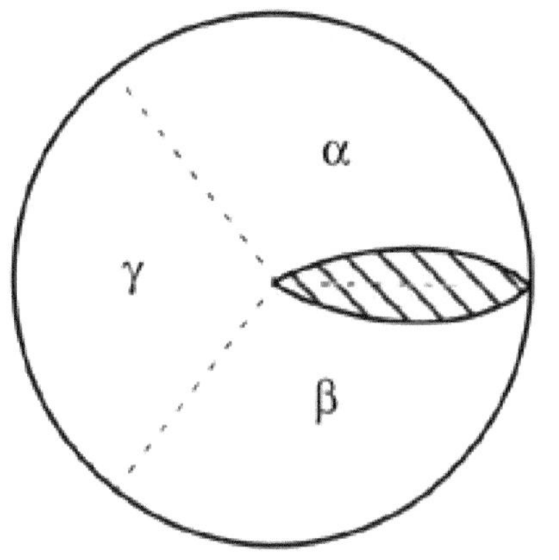

Figure 10-1. Softer Handoff

- Intercell or soft handoff.

- The mobile communicates with two or three sectors of different cells (see Fig). The base station that has the direct control of call processing during handoff is referred to as the primary base station.
- The primary base station can initiate the forward control message. A soft handoff uses considerably more network resources than the softer handoff.

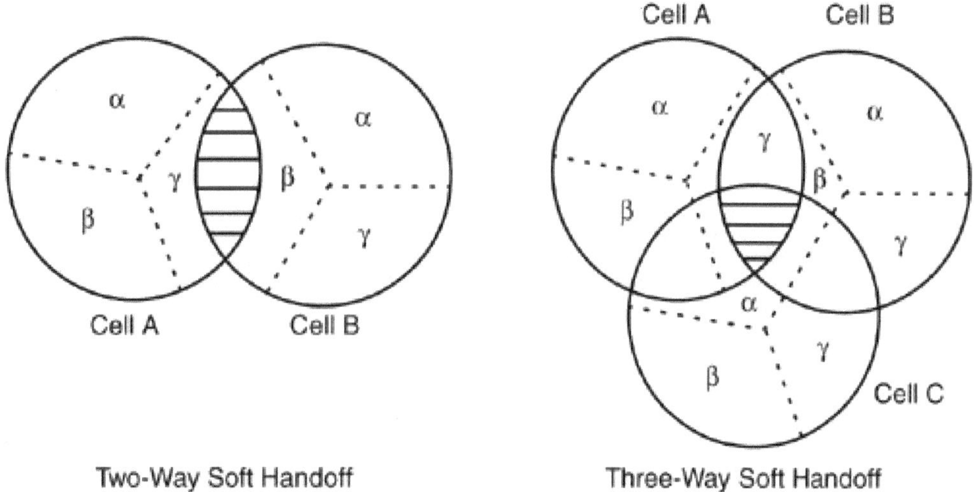

Figure 10-2. Soft Handoff

- Soft-softer handoff. The mobile communicates with two sectors of one cell and one sector of another cell. Network resources required for this type of handoff include the resources for a two-way soft handoff between cell A and B plus the resources for a softer handoff at cell B.

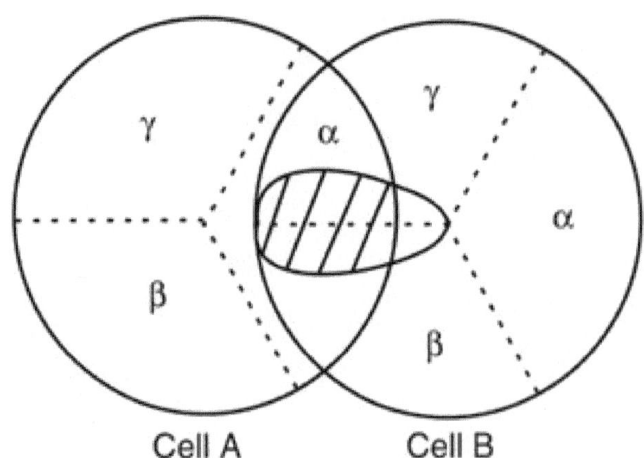

CDMA vs. GSM:

GSM (Global System for Mobile Communication) and **CDMA** (Code Division Multiple Access) are two dominant technologies for mobile communication.

1. Technology

- CDMAà is based on spread spectrum technology which makes the optimal use of available bandwidth. It allows each user to transmit over the entire frequency spectrum all the time.
- GSM àoperates on the wedge spectrum called a carrier. This carrier is divided into a number of time slots and each user is assigned a different time slot so that until the ongoing call is finished, no other subscriber can have access to this.

2. Security

- More security is provided in CDMA technology as compared with the GSM technology as encryption is inbuilt in the CDMA.
- A unique code is provided to every user and all the conversation between two users are encoded ensuring a greater level of security for CDMA users.
- The signal cannot be detected easily in CDMA as compared to the signals of GSM, which are concentrated in the narrow bandwidth. Therefore, the CDMA phone calls are more secure than the GSM calls.

3. Spectrum Frequencies

- The CDMA networkà operates in the frequency spectrum of CDMA 850 MHz and 1900 MHz
- GSM network àoperates in the frequency spectrum of GSM 850 MHz and 1900 MHz

4. Global Reach

- GSM à is in use over 80% of the world's mobile networks in over 210 countries as compared to CDMA.
- CDMAà is almost exclusively used in United States and some parts of Canada and Japan.

5. Data Transfer Rate

- CDMAà has faster data rate as compared to GSM as EVDO data transfer technology is used in CDMA which offers a maximum download speed of 2 mbps.
- GSM àuses EDGE data transfer technology that has a maximum download speed of 384 kbps which is slower as compared to CDMA. So CDMA is known to cover more area with fewer towers.

WIRELESS DATA:

- Data Transmission over wireless network is like CDMA 0r GSM is always Challenge.

CDMA protocol stacks in following layers:

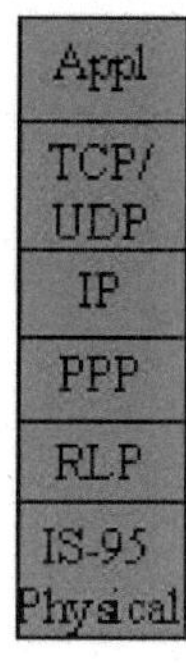

Application interface layer:

- It includes the interface between the data source in the mobile station and the transport layer.

Transport layer:

- The transport layer for CDMA asynchronous data and fax based on TCP.

Network layer:

- The transport layer for CDMA asynchronous data and fax based on IP.

Data link layer:
This Layer Uses PPP (Point-Point Protocol).

- The Link Control Protocol (LCP) is used for initial link establishment and for the negotiation of optional link capabilities.

Radio Link Layer(RLP):

- This layer provides octet stream service over the air.
- It is responsible for reducing the error rate over the forward or reverse channels.
- There is no direct relationship between PPP packet and the traffic channel frame.

THIRD GENERATION NETWORKS:
3G APPLICATIONS

- 3g operators are planning to make their money with mobile applications even when there might never be a single killer application.
- According to umts forum , 3g data services are subdivided into content connectivity and mobility, then further subdivided to create the following six services:

- Customised Infotainment
- Multimedia Messaging Service
- Mobile Intranet/Extranet Access
- Mobile Internet Access
- Location-based Services
- Rich Voice

3G applications can be divided into:

- Wireless Advertising

- Mobile Information
- Business Solutions
- Mobile Transactions
- Mobile Entertainment
- Person-to-Person Communications
- Bearer Entrance and Periodic

Different types of client allocations:

- Local
- Occasionally connected.
- Online
- Real-time.

3G specific applications:

- Personal applications.
- Content applications.
- Communication application.
- Productivity application.
- Business application.

Virtual Home Environment

- According to the 3GPP VHE specifications, the VHE Business model and the user perspec- tive are structured as shown in [1] (Figure 1 and Figure 2).

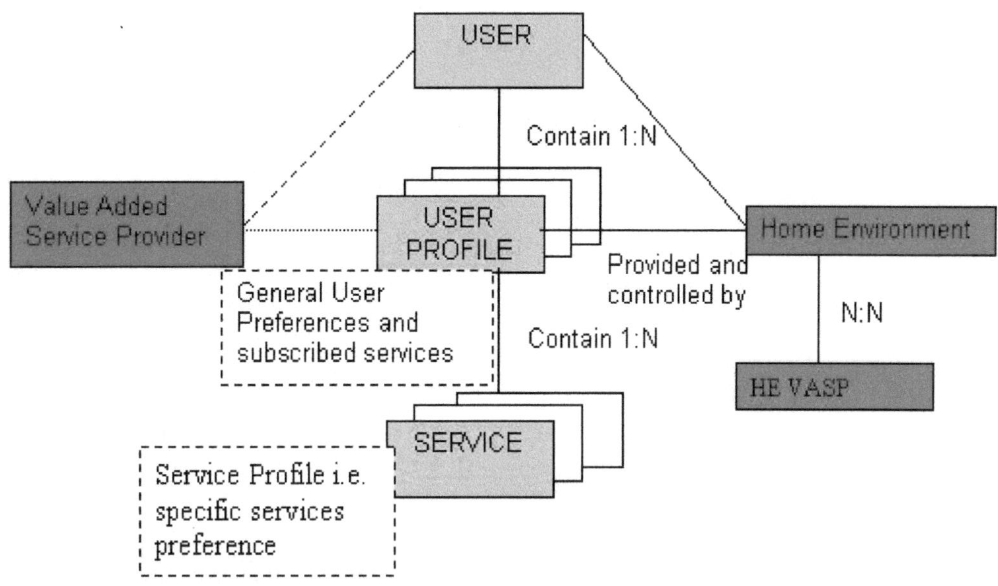

Figure 1 :VHE – Business Model

The entities shown in above fig have the following roles-functionalities:

- **User**: Subscribes accesses, customises and invokes services through the Home Environment and Value-Added Service Providers.
- **User Services Profile**: contains information on subscriber services, their status and service preferences. This is part of the User profile information, necessary to provide a user with a consistent, personalised service environment.
- **Services**: functionality content provided by the user.
- **Home Environment (HE)**: transparently provides services to the user in a managed way, possibly by collaborating with Home Environment – Value Added Service Providers (HE- VASPs).
- **Serving Network Operator**: Offers network connectivity, network-specific capabilities and services to the user vïa the HE. The serving network can be a Home Network (HN) or a Vis- ited (roamed) Network.
- **Value Added Service Provider (VASP)**: The user may access services directly from VASPs. Services obtained directly from VASPs are not managed by HIM and, therefore, are not part of the VHE service offered by the HE.
- **Home Environment – VASP (HE-VASP):** the user personalises and accesses the services provided by the HE-VASP through the HE. HE may allow HE-VASPs to access its service toolkits in the network.

IMT-2000:

It is a global standard for third generation systems, is defined by the International Telecommunication Union (ITU)

The main objectives for IMT-2000 are:

- High data rates: 144 Kbps/384 Kbps for high mobility users with full coverage; 2 Mbps for low mobility users with limited coverage.
- Capability for multimedia application and all mobile applications.
- high spectrum efficiency compared to existing systems
- high flexibility to introduce new services

- high degree of commonality of design worldwide
- use of a small pocket terminal with seamless global roaming

CDMA-2000:

- Cdma-Code Division Multiple Access.
- Spread Spectrum technique using Direct Sequence i.e. each data bit is represented (spread) by multiple bits in transmitted signal.
- Cdma2000-multi carrier mode Cdma
- It supports data rates both circuit and packet switched of 9.6kbps to 2 Mbps.
- Operates in wide range of environments
    - Outdoor Mega cells(cells 35km radius)
    - Outdoor macro cells(1-35 km radius)
    - Indoor/outdoor micro cells(1km radius)
- Indoor/outdoor Pico cells(<50-m radius)
- Cdma2000 can be deployed in
    - Indoor/Outdoor environment
    - Wireless Local Loops
    - Vehicular Environments
    - Mixed Vehicular & Indoor / Outdoor Environments
- Cdma2000 services support
    - Overlay configuration
    - Backward compatibility to TIA/EIA-95B signaling & network
    - Graceful & gradual upgrade from 2G to 3 G systems
    - Common channels with an underlay TIA/EIA-95B system during transition periods

FIXED WIRELESS:

- *Fixed wireless* refers to wireless devices or systems that are situated in fixed locations, such as an office or home, as opposed to devices that are mobile, such as cell phones and PDAs.
- Fixed wireless devices normally derive their electrical power from utility mains, as opposed to portable wireless devices that normally derive their power from batteries.
- The point-to-point signal transmissions occur through the air over a terrestrial microwave platform rather than through copper or fiber cables;
- Fixed wireless does not require satellite feeds or local phone service.
- The advantages of fixed wireless include the ability to connect with users in remote areas without the need for laying new cables and the capacity for broad bandwidth that is not impeded by fiber or cable capacities.

WIRELESS LAN:

Introduction

- A **wireless local area network (WLAN)** links two or more devices using some wireless distribution method (typically spread-spectrum or OFDM radio), and usually providing a connection through an access point to the wider Internet.

- This gives users the mobility to move around within a local coverage area and still be connected to the network.
- Most modern WLANs are based on IEEE 802.11 standards, marketed under the Wi-Fi brand name.

WIRELESS LAN ADVANTAGES:

- Mobility
- Installation in difficult-to-wire areas
- Increased reliability
- Reduced installation time
- Long term cost savings

1. Mobility:

- Easy to move physically while using an appliance, such as a handheld PC or data collector pda.
- Many jobs require workers to be mobile, such as inventory clerks, healthcare workers, policemen, and emergency care specialist.
- Mobility result to mobile application
- Mobile applications requiring wireless networking include those that depend on real-time access to data – usually stored in centralized databases.

2. Installation in difficult-to-wire areas:

- The implementation of wireless networks offers many tangible cost savings when performing installations in difficult to wire areas.
- E.g. two building that separate by river/road/railroad track (fig 1.2). A wireless lan may be much more economical than installing physical cable or leasing communications circuits, such as T1 service or 56kbps lines.
- To apply wireless connection in this situation may be cost a lot of money. But it will benefit in the long run. (long term investment)

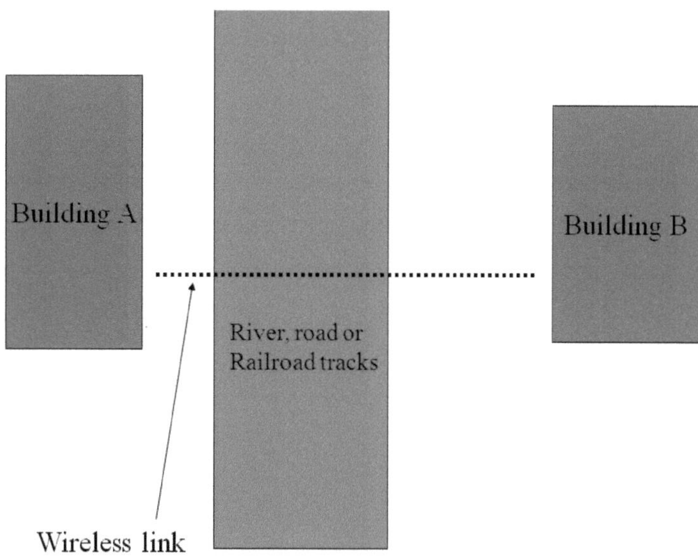

3.Increased reliability:

- A problem inherent to wired network is downtime due to cable faults. E.g. moisture erodes metallic conductors via water intrusion during storms and accidental spillage or leakage of liquids.
- An advantage of wireless networking, therefore, results from the use of less cable. This reduces the downtime of the network and the costs related with replacing cables.

4. Reduced installation time:

- The deployment of wireless network greatly reduces the need for cable installation, making the network available for use much sooner.
- But the installation of cabling is often a time-consuming activity.

IEEE 802.11 STANDARDS:

- Somewhere in 1997, IEEE finalized the initial standard for wireless LANs: IEEE 802.11. This standard specifies a 2.4Ghz operating frequency with data rates of 1 and 2 Mbps. The initial 802.11 standard defines two forms of spread spectrum modulation: frequency hopping (802.11 FHSS) and direct sequence (802.11 DSSS).
- In late 1999, the IEEE published two supplements to the 802.11 standard. 802.11a and 802.11b.

Standards are:

1. IEEE 802.11 à standard for wireless LAN operation at data rates up to 2 mbps in the 2.1 GHZ.
2. IEEE 802.11a à standard for wireless LAN operation at data rates up to 54mbps in the 5 GHZ.
3. IEEE 802.11b à standard for wireless LAN operation at data rates up to 11 mbps in the 2.4 GHZ.
4. IEEE 802.11g à high-rate extension to 802.11b allowing for data rates up to 54 mbps in the 2.4 GHz.
5. IEEE 802.15.1à Wireless personal Area network standard based on the Bluetooth specification
6. IEEE.802.1x àPort-based network access control defines infrastructure to provide authenticating and authorizing devices.
7. IEEE 802.11g --> is a new standard, describing a wireless networking method for WLANs that operates in the 2.4 radio band (ISM frequency band). Industrial-Scientific-Medical

802.11 ARCHITECTURE:

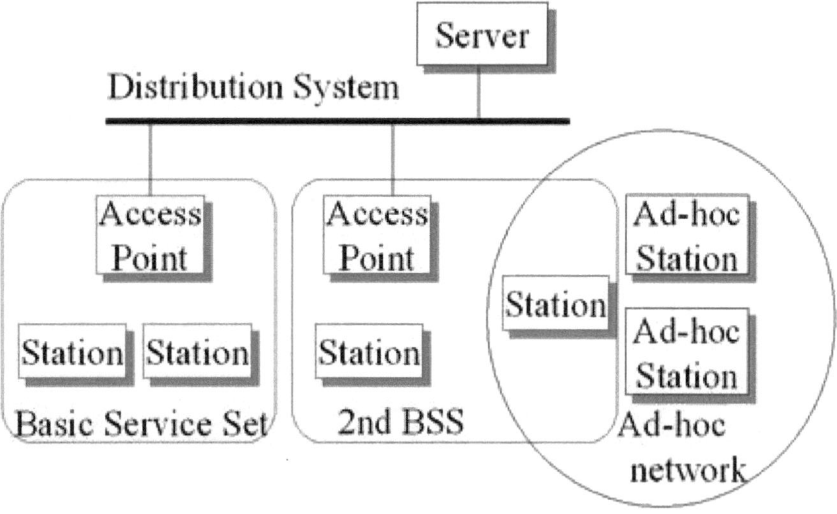

IEEE 802.11 LAYERS DESCRIPTION:

- There are three layers in PHs

  1. Frequency hopping spread spectrum (FHSS).
  2. Direct Sequence Spread Spectrum (DSSS).
  3. Infrared.

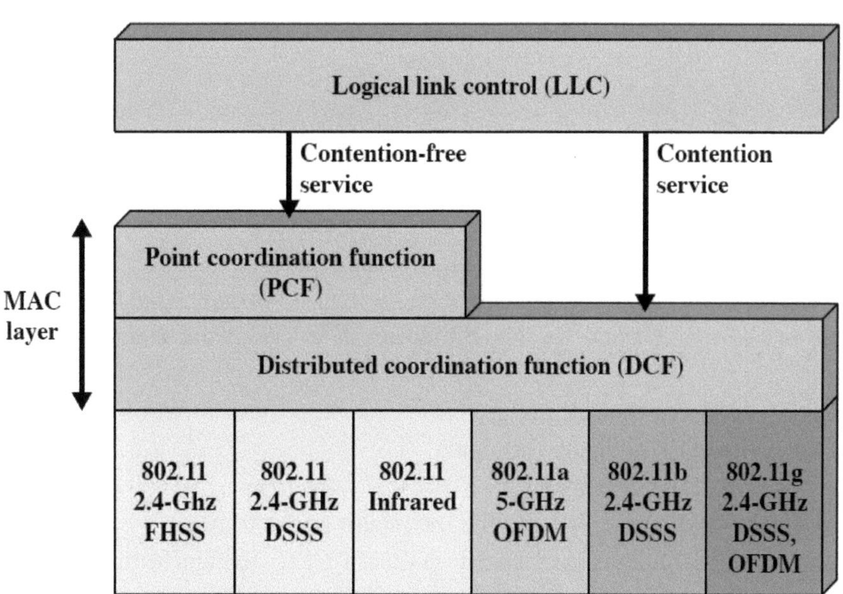

Enter Caption

PHYSICAL LAYER ARCHITECTURE:

Two sub layers:

1. **PLCP(Physical layer convergence procedure):**

- It is responsible for Carrier Sense(CS)part of the (CSMA/CA) protocol.
- It prepares MAC protocol for data transmission.
- It also delivers incoming frames from the wireless medium to the MAC layer.

2. **PMD(Physical Medium Dependant):**

- It provides actual transmission of physical layer entities through the wireless media.
- It provides modulation and demodulation of transmission.

FREQUENCY HOPPING SPREAD SPECTRUM (FHSS):

It carries the clocking information to synchronize the receiver clock with the clock of the transmission packet.
The fields of FHSS are:

1. SYNC à it is made up of alternate 0's and 1's. The bit pattern is to synchronize the clock of the receiver.
2. Start Frame Delimiter à it indicates the beginning of the frame and the content of the field is fixed.
3. PSDU length Word (PLW)à it specifies the length of the PSDU in octets.
4. PLCP Signaling (PSF)à it contains information about the data rate of the fields from PSDU.
5. Header Error Checkà it contains CRC (Cyclic Redundancy Check).

DIRECT SEQUENCE SPREAD SPECTRUM (DSSS):

- Each bit in original signal is represented by multiple bits in the transmitted signal
- Spreading code spreads signal across a wider frequency band
    - Spread is in direct proportion to the number of bits used
- One technique combines digital information stream with the spreading code bit stream using exclusive-OR

DSSS PLCP:
It is responsible for synchronizing and receiving the data bits correctly.
The fields are:

1. SYNC à it is made up of alternate 0's and 1's. The bit pattern is to synchronize the clock of the receiver with the received frame.
2. Start Frame Delimiter à it indicates the beginning of the frame and the content of the field is fixed.
3. Signalà the receiver must use to demodulate the signal.
4. Serviceà this field is not used and is usually 0.
5. Lengthàit contains unsigned 16-bit integer indicting the length of the frame.
6. Frame Check Sequenceà it is 16-bit checksum based on CCITT CRC -16 algorithms.

PMD Sub layer:
Under the direction of the PLCP, the Physical Medium Dependent (PMD)
Sub layer provides transmission and reception of Physical layer data units

Between two stations via the wireless medium.

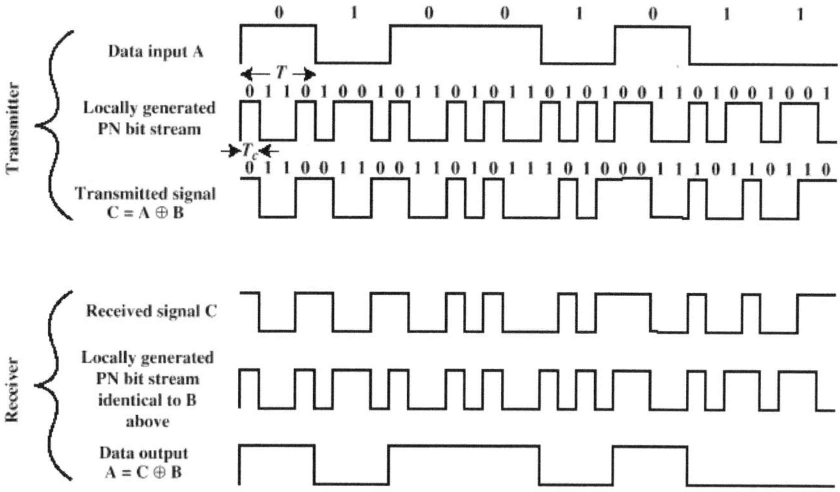

MOBILITY IN WIRELESS LAN:

- When a station wants to access an existing BSS(either sleep mode, after power setup), it needs to synchronize information from the AP.
- The station can get the information by

1. *Passive Scanning*: à the station just waits to receive a frame from AP.
2. *Active Scanning* àthe station tries to locate an Access Point by transmitting request frames waits for response.

The authentication process:

- Once the station is located an AP and decides to join its BSS,it goes through authentication process.
- This is an interchange of authentication information between the AP and the station.

The Association process:

- Once it is authenticated , it can exchange of information about the stations and BSS capabilities
- It allows the DSS à to know about the current position of the station.

Roaming:

- It is a process moving from one cell to another without losing connection.

EG: On a packet based LAN system, the transition from cell to cell may be performed between packet transmissions, as opposed to telephony where the transition may occur during a phone conversation.

DEPLOYING WIRELESS LAN

CONFIGURING THE WIRELESS LAN:

1. Connect to the Internet

Make sure that your Internet connection and your DSL or cable modem are working. Your wireless network depends on this connection.

2. Connect your wireless router

These are the steps for connecting a stand-alone wireless router to your DSL modem or cable modem. If you have a modem router, follow your ISP's instructions for connecting your network.

- First, locate your cable modem or DSL modem and unplug it to turn it off.

- Next, connect your wireless router to your modem. Your modem should stay connected directly to the Internet. Later, after you've hooked everything up, your computer will wirelessly connect to your router, and the router will send communications through your modem to the Internet

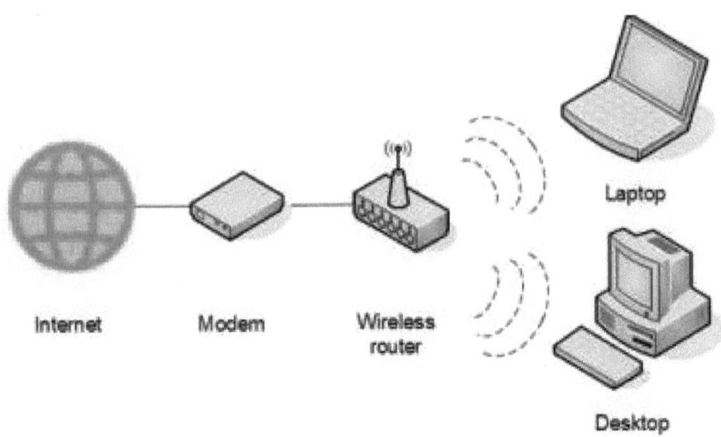

3. *Configure your wireless router:*

- Using the network cable that came with your wireless router, you should temporarily connect your computer to one of the open network ports on your wireless router .Next, open Internet Explorer and type in the URL or address to configure your router.

4. Connect your computers, printers, and other devices to the wireless network

You can connect multiple computers, printers, and many other peripheral devices, such as an Xbox, Xbox 360, TV, cell phone, iTouch, or iPad, to your network

5. Share files, printers, and more

Now that your computers and devices are connected, you can begin sharing files, printers, games, and much more. One of the top reasons for setting up a home network is to share a printer.

MOBILE ADHOC NETWORKS AND SENSOR NETWORKS :

MOBILE ADHOC NETWORKS:

- A mobile ad hoc Network (MANET) is an autonomous system of mobile stations connected by wireless lings to form network.
- It is modeled as arbitrary graph.
- ad hoc Networks are

1. Peer-to-peer.
2. Multi-hop networks.

- Communication link could be either symmetric or asymmetric.

Challenges to design a wireless network:

1. *Dynamic Topology* ànodes are free to move in an arbitrary fashion.
2. *Limited security* àit is vulnerable to attack as by design any node should be able to join or leave the network any time.
3. *Bandwidth limited* à because there is no backbone to handle or multiplex higher bandwidth.
4. *Routing*àit is complex depends on many factors such as finding the routing path, selection of routers, topology.

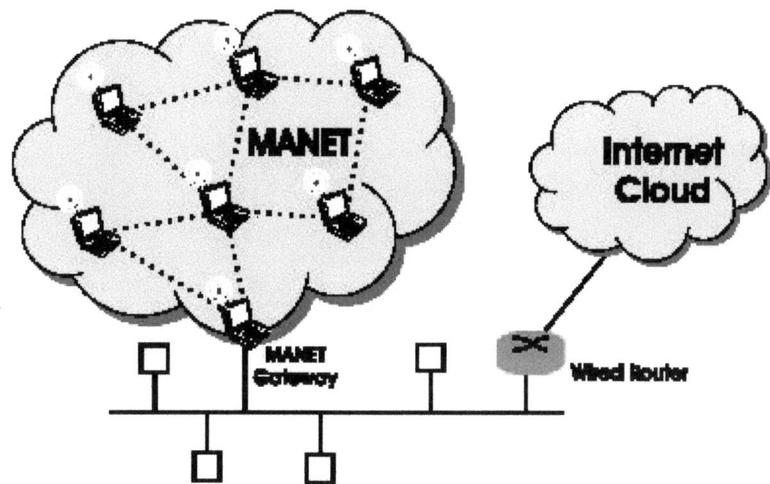

- Formed dynamically through the cooperation of independent nodes
- Nodes do not have any pre-specified roles
- Nodes make decision independently based on the current network situation
- Nodes are expected to behave as routers
- As routers, nodes must assist in discovery and maintenance of network routes

WIRELESS SENSOR NETWORKS:

- It is a class of ad hoc networks.
- Sensor networks are very useful in unpredictable, unreliable environment.
- It primarily data collection network.
- It is collection of low cost, low power disposable devices.
- It may not have any power source other than small batteries.

WIRELESS LAN SECURITY:

- **Wireless security** is the prevention of unauthorized access or damage to computers using wireless networks.
- The most common types of wireless security are Wired Equivalent Privacy (WEP) and Wi-Fi Protected Access (WPA).
- WEP is a notoriously weak security standard.

- The password it uses can often be cracked in a few minutes with a basic laptop computer and widely available software tools. WEP is an old IEEE 802.11 standard from 1999 which was outdated in 2003 by WPA or Wi-Fi Protected Access.
- WPA was a quick alternative to improve security over WEP. The current standard is WPA2; some hardware cannot support WPA2 without firmware upgrade or replacement.
- WPA2 uses an encryption device which encrypts the network with a 256 bit key; the longer key length improves security over WEP.

- Good cryptography allows secure communications over unsecured medium
- Follow best practice cryptographic principles

  q. Strong authentication
  q. Strong encryption

- Strong authentication is often overlooked
- Well established secure authentication methods all use SSL or TLS tunnels
- TLS is the successor of SSL
- SSL has been used for nearly a decade in E-Commerce
- SSL or TLS requires Digital Certificates
- Digital Certificates usually involves some form of PKI and Certificate management
- Intent to protect link between wireless client and (assumed) more secure wired network
- Similar to a VPN and provides server authentication, client authentication, data privacy, and integrity using per session and per user short life keys
- Simpler and more cost efficient than a VPN
- Cross-platform support and interoperability, not highly scalable, though
- Supports Linux and Windows

3G vs WIFI

ABOUT WI – FI

- WI – Fi is the wireless technology mostly used by mobile users to stay connected to the outer world through internet.
- It is mostly used by for office use, or at home. It uses IEEE standard. IEEE 802.11 is commonly known as wireless fidelity.
- Advantages of this technology are since its wireless it reduces the cost for cable connections.
- It is easily available in market.
- A person using WI – FI on laptop can move from one place to another or we can say from one access point to another with ease.
- It uses global set of standards so that the user using it can carry the same WI – Fi from one place to another.
- Disadvantages are the power consumption is more for the devices using this technology. T
- The use of Wi – Fi can be interrupted by using some other device like cordless phone.

ABOUT 3G

- As the name suggest 3G is the third generation technology. In early years it was also known as ITU IMT – 2000 it was started in 1980's.
- The main objective behind the establishment of 3G was to develop a technology which will provide a worldwide standard and a faster data access.

- It uses three different technologies WCDM (in Europe), CDMA2000 (North America), TD – SCDMA (in china).
- GSM uses 200 KHz of bandwidth and provide a speed of 9.6kbps. GPRS uses 200 kHz of bandwidth and 40 Kbps of data speed.
- 3G works on three basic things spread spectrum, direct sequence, and frequency hopping. It uses W – CDMA which increases data transmission rate in GSM. Advantages of 3G are it is spread over larger area so easy to access. It is cheaper. Disadvantages are cost of upgrading bas station is higher, power required for the device is higher, roaming has not been yet demonstrated.

9 798886 410051

Printed by Libri Plureos GmbH in Hamburg,
Germany